ANTHROPOLOGICAL PAPERS

MUSEUM OF ANTHROPOLOGY, UNIVERSITY OF MICHIGAN

NO. 33

OHIO HOPEWELL CERAMICS

An Analysis of the Extant Collections

BY

OLAF H. PRUFER

ANN ARBOR

THE UNIVERSITY OF MICHIGAN, 1968

ISBN (print): 978-1-949098-14-3
ISBN (ebook): 978-1-949098-72-3

Browse all of our books at
sites.lsa.umich.edu/archaeology-books.

Order our books from the University of Michigan
Press at www.press.umich.edu.

For permissions, questions, or manuscript queries,
contact Museum publications by email at umma-
pubs@umich.edu or visit the Museum website at
lsa.umich.edu/ummaa.

CONTENTS

I. Introduction 1

II. Methodology 4

III. Definitions 7

IV. Sites 16

- Harness 16
- Rockhold 29
- Hopewell 31
- Ater 40
- Ginther 41
- Tremper 45
- Mound City 50
- Seip 61
- Fort Ancient 88
- Fort Hill 90
- Marriott-1 92
- Turner 96
- Russell Brown 139

V. Discussion 148

References 154

I
INTRODUCTION

ONE of the least known aspects of the Hopewellian Phase in Ohio is the nature of the ceramics associated with Hopewellian sites. To date, only two statements on such pottery have appeared in print. In 1945 Dr. James B. Griffin offered a brief discussion of Ohio Hopewell pottery (Griffin, 1945), and recently Prufer and McKenzie (1965) have dealt with the ceramic remains from the McGraw site in Ross County, Ohio. The latter study has led to the definition of a number of pottery types, subsumed under three ceramic series: Scioto, Hopewellian and Southeastern. This study also provided a sketchy analysis of ceramic remains from other Hopewellian localities in Ohio.

In view of the known significance of pottery as a cultural and chronological index in the prehistory of the Eastern United States, it may seem surprising that the ceramic remains from the resplendent Hopewell sites have been dealt with in such a cavalier manner. The actual references to pottery in diverse site reports are woefully inadequate, if not irrelevant, and they hardly fill more than a dozen pages. The reasons for this situation are largely historical. All major excavations of Hopewell sites were carried out between *circa* 1880 and 1930. The significance of ceramics ("fictile arts") was then barely recognized. At best, pottery was proof for yet another "art" mastered by the "primitive mound-builders." Even in 1931, when Shetrone and Greenman published their report on Seip-1, the only significant division that was made resulted from the recognition that "ceremonial pottery" (Hopewellian and Southeastern Series) was different and distinct from "utility ware" (Scioto Series).

The almost total disregard for ceramics reflected in the literature has two corollaries. First, it led to a complete neglect of recording the provenience of sherds, not only within mounds, but, in several instances, even between mounds of a given site. Second, this attitude was perpetuated in some Museums to the extent that ceramics from a given site of numerous mounds were simply lumped under the same accession number—even when detailed provenience unit data were available. In addition, they were thrown into single storage boxes.

There is also internal evidence to the effect that in a number of instances the less spectacular Scioto Series sherds were summarily thrown away. This brings us to the question of the reliability of the percentage counts for the diverse ceramic series. This matter has recently been discussed at some length by Prufer and McKenzie (1965). For present purposes the evidence need merely be summarized.

It is clear that, with the exception of the Turner and Marriot-1 material *in toto*, and the Harness material, to the extent to which it was excavated by Putnum—in short all the ceramics unearthed by the Peabody Museum—no great reliance can be placed upon available sherds from all those sites excavated before 1931, that is, during the period ending with the second campaign at the Seip earthworks.

This restricts reliable counts for the following sites: Ater, Rockhold, Fort Hill, Fort Ancient (Morgan's excavations), McGraw, Brown's Bottom, and the Russell Brown mounds. Presumably the Esch material should also be included here.

A second factor that relates to data reliability is connected with the gradual whittling away of certain site collections due to dispersal of material on loan or in the form of type collections. Especially the Seip material has been affected by this. Sample collections of preponderantly "classic" sherds are dispersed in several institutions. For purposes of the present analysis it did not prove possible to track down all these sherds. Again, internal evidence indicates that other ceramic assemblages were also thus affected. It is in this manner only, that a number of discrepancies between our own analysis and that summarily presented by Griffin (1945) can be explained. These differences, discussed by Prufer and McKenzie (1965), are still valid, even though a further search for material after the initial analysis by Prufer in 1962-63 has produced additional sherds from a number of sites.

The present analysis covers all available ceramics from Ohio Hopewell sites, with the exception of the pottery from McGraw, Brown's Bottom, the recent Mound City material, and the Esch mounds. The first two collections have been dealt with elsewhere (Prufer and McKenzie, 1965; Blank, 1965). The Mound City sherds found by James Brown during the 1963 excavations will be dealt with at a later date; and the material from the Esch mounds will be published within the framework of the overall site report.

My gratitude is due a number of institutions and individuals. First and foremost, I wish to acknowledge the National Science Foundation for a grant (GS-4) which made this work possible, and

Case Institute of Technology which in many ways supported this enterprise. Among the many individuals who contributed time, help, and advice I should like to thank Dr. John O. Brew, Director of the Peabody Museum of Harvard University, and Mr. Raymond S. Baby, Curator of Archaeology at the Ohio State Museum, for generously making available to me the extensive collections in their institutions. I also wish to thank Miss Elizabeth E. Baldwin of Western Michigan University, Kalamazoo, and Miss Karen Kerner of Columbia University, for their very substantial help in analyzing the Turner and Harness ceramics. I am also beholden to Dr. James B. Griffin of the University of Michigan, and to my colleague Dr. Douglas H. McKenzie of Case Institute of Technology, for their warm responses to my often tiresome queries on the secrets of what has jocularly been styled "psychoceramics." Finally, I wish to acknowledge Mr. Robert Kielkowicz, then of the Cleveland Museum of Natural History, and Mr. Charles Covic of Case Institute of Technology, for their photographic skills in preparing the illustrations.

Olaf H. Prufer
May 1, 1965

II

METHODOLOGY

This study constitutes an attempt at presenting an analysis of all available ceramics from Ohio Hopewell sites. It is intended to be a contribution to the little known subject of Middle Woodland pottery in Ohio. Furthermore, it should prove useful to the establishment of a ceramic chronology for this period, and to current efforts of elucidating the general, cultural, and specifically ceramic relationships between various "hopewellianized" areas in the Eastern United States.

A first step in this direction was taken with the detailed analysis of the ceramics from the single-component McGraw site in Ross County, Ohio (Prufer and McKenzie, 1965). This led to the recognition of three distinct ceramic series, each of which appears to have a separate cultural genesis. These three units were named Scioto Series, Hopewellian Series, and Southeastern Series. Within each of these it was possible to define a number of pottery types as follows:

I. Scioto Series
   1. McGraw Cord-marked
   2. McGraw Plain

II. Hopewellian Series
   1. Chillicothe Rocker-stamped
      A. Plain-rocked
      B. Plain long-rocked ("Pike")
      C. Dentate long-rocked ("Pike")

III. Southeastern Series
   1. Turner Simple-stamped

The present analysis shows that these series and types are valid beyond the McGraw site. Their definitions need no modifications, with the exception of a certain minor terminological change: since it has been possible to establish a second simple-stamped pottery type within the Southeastern Series, the type defined at McGraw should now be called Turner Simple-stamped *A*, whereas the new type has been named Turner Simple-stamped *B*.

In order to keep the length of the present study to a minimum consistent with clarity, the already established type definitions will not be presented here; the reader is referred to the McGraw site report for all necessary details (Prufer and McKenzie, 1965). Only such departures from the type descriptions as have been noted from site to site, and a few other pertinent observations will be given here. Thus, wherever there are no comments on the established types in the following analyses, it should be assumed that their particular representatives at the various sites are in all respects identical and consistent with the original type definition.

On the basis of the present analysis it seems possible to define, at least provisionally, one further ceramic series, two types, one subtype, and one provisional type. In each case the criteria for establishing the unit were not so much absolute numbers of sherds, as their constant recurrence at several sites, and the fact that their diverse defining attributes were quite distinct and always present. This means, that a number of potential types were left undefined, even though numerically they were more common than some of the defined types. For example, the Southeastern Series Plain sherds were left undefined in any formal sense, because one can never be certain whether rim and neck sherds classed as "plain" did not, in fact, belong to simple-stamped vessels on which the decorations were restricted to the body only. In order to define such a type, far more sherds would have been required than those at present available. The new units, which will be described in detail below, have been named as follows:

1. Series: Miami Series (provisional)
2. Types: Hopewellian Series, Seip Plain
   Southeastern Series, Turner Simple-stamped *B*
   Southeastern Series, Turner Check-stamped (provisional)
3. Subtypes: Hopewellian Series, Chillicothe Rocker-stamped, Dentate-rocked

The remaining sherds which could not be typed, were grouped according to their obvious series affiliations and named purely descriptively according to their most obvious attributes (example: Southeastern Series, Untyped Complicated-stamped). In those cases where series affiliation could not be determined, this is stated as follows: Unknown Series, Untyped Incised. In the present terminology for Ohio, I have only retained one name specifically devised for another area (Illinois). This is Brangenberg Plain. The few sherds of this type are so distinctive and so obviously identical with their Illinoian counterparts that retension of the established type name seemed justified.

As much as possible, the ceramics were analyzed by provenience units. The crudest data stem from sherds which were not originally kept separate, even as to the particular mounds within a given group. Such data are discussed under the name of the site, with the added notation General. Where data on mound provenience are available, this is indicated by the number of the mound affixed to the discussion. Occasionally, even more specific provenience data could be determined. In such cases the ceramics are discussed by provenience units, though in the overall statistics the mound unit is the lowest that was considered, because our present knowledge did not show a single case where pottery from a specific within-mound provenience unit differed from that of any other unit of the same mound. Still, in the detailed tabulations to follow, all provenience units are kept separate.

All sherds were examined as to the temper; rim and body thickness were measured throughout. In the case of large samples from single provenience units, and consisting of sherds of the same type, random samples of at least 25 sherds were measured and taken to represent the true values. For control purposes in such cases a second random sample was measured. The metric values are given in millimeters and fractions of millimeters. In the tabulations the range measurements of a given sample are always presented without fractional values; means are given with fractional values. For all sites, mounds, and features which yielded ceramics, all relevant published references to pottery are given; similarly, all available data on such ceramics found in the various Museum catalogues are presented as well.

All references to temper should be obvious and self-explanatory, except for the notation "mixed temper." This refers to an approximately equal mixture of grit and limestone particles. The qualitative terms "fine," "medium," and "coarse" for particle size denote the following: fine temper means average particle size up to 2 mm in diameter; medium ranges from 2 to 5 mm; and coarse exceeds 5 mm. Particles with diameters of less than 1 mm occasionally occur. Such temper is referred to as extremely fine.

Illustrations are grouped for each site by series and types, with detailed indications as to provenience units.

III

DEFINITIONS

MIAMI SERIES (No types; provisional)

This is a highly tentative series which is set up here merely because the sixteen component sherds are very distinctive and appear to be closely related if not identical with Weaver material from Illinois. Certainly, these sherds do not fit into any of the established ceramic series of Ohio Woodland. They are characterized predominantly by rim sherds with double or multiple rows of usually hemiconical punctations or deep exterior bosses. The rims generally are straight-vertical. A single cord-marked rim sherd from Rockhold-2 has the cord-wrapped-stick stamping shown on the Weaver vessels as illustrated by Griffin (1952: Pl. XXXVII). None of these sherds can be affiliated with the Scioto Series either during the Hopwellian Phase, or in the subsequent Peters Phase. The new tentative series name has been derived from the Miami River drainage, where the majority of the component sherds (14) were found at the Turner site. In addition, a single sherd was found at Rockhold, and another at Seip. Only posterity can validate this series.

HOPEWELLIAN SERIES, Seip Plain

GENERAL DATA

New type not previously described. The type name was derived from the site with the largest number of sherds. Present definition is based upon finds from five sites: Seip (87), Turner (2), Harness (2), Hopewell (6), and Mound City (2).

Body sherds, grit:	78
limestone:	2
Rim sherds, grit:	20
	100

PASTE

Method of manufacture: Coiled.

Temper: Generally extremely fine to fine grit or, rarely, limestone. Particle density is low.

Texture: Uncontorted and unlaminated. Clay is very fine and well mixed. At Seip a few sherds are made of an orange, almost white, sugary clay. The quality is always excellent; the sherds are not crumbly.

Hardness: No measurements taken (see Prufer and McKenzie, 1965:18). Generally quite hard.

Color: Various shades of brown and red-brown. At Seip many sherds have shades from yellow-buff to orange-brown. The very light colored sherds here are the same as those made of the light colored, sugary, clay.

SURFACE TREATMENT

All vessels are completely undecorated. The surfaces are invariably polished or smoothed. At Seip, this treatment had its highest development; here the polishing often creates the impression of a glossy sheen. In the case of bowls in particular, and interior rim areas in general, this carries over onto the interior surfaces.

FORM

Rim: Straight rims are associated with bowls. In addition there are recurvate, *S*-shaped rims and thickened Hopewell rims without any decorations.

Lip: Lips are round or flat. All bowls have flat lips.

Body: Open bowls and globular vessels have been noted. All vessels appear to be rather small; two vessels proved to be lobate.

Base: Bases appear to be round.

Thickness: Body sherds: All but two sherds were measured:

Range:	3-6 mm
Mean:	4.2 mm

Rim sherds: The entire sample was measured:

Range:	3-8 mm
Mean:	5.7 mm

Appendages: None.

GEOGRAPHICAL RANGE

This type is not common in Ohio. It does however, occur throughout the classic Hopewellian area of southern Ohio.

CHRONOLOGICAL POSITION

The type occupies the middle and late ranges of the Hopewellian Phase in Ohio. It seems most abundant during the middle period as exemplified by Seip and Hopewell. If the few curious stray sherds from Tremper should turn out to belong to this type, the temporal range should be extended into the early period of the local Hopewellian Phase.

PROBABLE RELATIONSHIPS

Apart from its obvious relationship to the Hopewellian Series in general, Seip Plain is very similar to its equivalent types in other areas, notably Illinois.

SOUTHEASTERN SERIES, Turner Simple-stamped *B*

GENERAL DATA

New type not previously described. The type is named after the Turner site in Hamilton County, Ohio, which yielded the largest series of simple-stamped sherds of this type. Present analysis is based upon samples from the following sites: Turner (82), Fort Ancient (5), Fort Hill (1), Ginther (6), Tremper (3), Seip (25), and Mound City (8):

Body sherds, sand:	118
Rim sherds, sand:	13
	131

Multiple sherds representing a single vessel are listed as one sherd. Included in the above are 15 tetrapods representing as many vessels.

PASTE

Method of manufacture: Coiled.

Temper: Fine, occasionally medium sand. Particle density is low to medium.

Texture: Fine, generally uncontorted and unlaminated. The texture is homogeneous and sandy. Clays are well mixed.

Hardness: No measurements were taken (see Prufer and McKenzie, 1965:18). Turner Simple-stamped *B* and related sand-tempered types proved to be the hardest and least crumbly ceramics associated with Ohio Hopewell sites. In some cases the sherds have an almost stone-like quality.

Color: The overwhelming majority of all sherds are grey-black in color; the remainder are brown-grey. Core color is similar to surface color.

SURFACE TREATMENT

The exterior surfaces are decorated with simple-stamping produced by means of a grooved paddle. Sometimes the decorations overlap. In contrast to the stamping on Turner Simple-stamped *A*, the stamps here are very close together, and rather shoddy in appearance; in many cases the effect is almost that of coarse brushing. However, it is always possible to distinguish this treatment from real brushing. In many cases the decorations cover the vessel body only, being separated from the plain neck and rim by a band of angular or hemiconical punctates. There are, however, some cases where simple-stamping reaches up to the lip. Smoothing of the decorations is very rare, and even then only slight.

FORM

Rim: The rims are excurvate and flaring, occasionally straight.

Lip: Lips are always rounded. Usually they are thin, occasionally "knife-edged."

Body: Small- to medium-sized globular vessels are the rule. A single complete vessel from Mound City-13, indicates that sometimes these can be almost miniaturized.

Base: The data seem to indicate that overwhelmingly this type is characterized by tetrapodal bases. The individual tetrapods are stubby and short, rarely exceeding 15 mm in length.

Thickness: Body sherds: The total sample was measured:

Range:	3-9 mm
Mean:	4.2 mm

Rim sherds: The total sample was measured:

Range:	3-6 mm
Mean:	4.8 mm

Appendages: Tetrapods. Some of these were added after completion of the vessel, while in other cases they were molded directly in the clay of the body.

GEOGRAPHICAL RANGE

Within Ohio, Turner Simple-stamped *B* appears throughout the classic area of southern Ohio, though it is not present at all sites.

CHRONOLOGICAL POSITION

Throughout the entire local sequence of the Hopewellian Phase.

PROBABLE RELATIONSHIPS

Turner Simple-stamped *B* does not appear to be indigenous to Ohio. Its closest relatives seem to be Deptford Simple-stamped and Mossy Oak Simple-stamped (Griffin and Sears, 1950). This is primarily based on temper and decoration, and only secondarily on form. Also, this type is related in terms of form and decoration, but not temper, to Turner Simple-stamped A, and, by extension, to Paintsville Simple-stamped of Kentucky Adena (Haag, 1942*a*), and Bluff Creek Simple-stamped of the Copena complex (Haag, 1942*b*).

SOUTHEASTERN SERIES, Turner Check-stamped (provisional type)

GENERAL DATA

Provisional type not previously described. In the absence of any identifiable rim sherds, this series of sherds can not be accorded full type status. On the other hand the sherds are very uniform and distinctive, as well as quite numerous; they should not just be relegated to a residual unclassified category. Present definition is based upon material from five sites: Turner (78), Harness (19), Fort Hill (1), Seip (1), and McGraw (1):

Body sherds, grit:	62
limestone:	38
	100

PASTE

Method of manufacture: Coiled.

Temper: For both grit and limestone the temper particles range from fine to medium. Particle density is variable, though generally moderate.

Texture: Uncontorted, unlaminated and homogeneous.

Hardness: No measurements taken (see Prufer and McKenzie, 1965: 18). Hardness range varies from crumbly and fairly soft, to well-fired and moderately hard.

Color: Most sherds are reddish-brown, grading into dark dirty-brown. Occasional sherds are dirty buff. The reddish tinge is characteristic.

SURFACE TREATMENT

All sherds are covered with check-stamping produced by a carved paddle. The individual check-stamps are overwhelmingly small, generally not exceeding 4 mm square. They are very regular. Overlapping has only rarely been noted. Smoothing is common and occasionally heavy.

FORM

Rim: No data.

Lip: No data.

Body: Apparently medium to large globular vessels.

Base: Apparently round.

Thickness: Body sherds: The entire sample was measured:

Range:	3-11 mm
Mean:	4.8 mm

The overwhelming impression is that of thin-bodied vessels.

Appendages: None.

GEOGRAPHICAL RANGE

Throughout the classic Hopewell area of southern Ohio.

CHRONOLOGICAL POSITION

Thus far Turner Check-stamped seems to cover the middle and late periods of the Ohio Hopewellian Phase.

EXTERNAL RELATIONSHIPS

Occasional sherds, apparently similar to this type, occur in Kentucky Adena. More substantially, this provisional type seems to be fairly closely related to Wright Check-stamped in the middle south (Haag, 1942*b*), and, by extension, to Wheeler Check-stamped in the lower Mississippi Valley (Phillips, Ford, and Griffin, 1951).

HOPEWELLIAN SERIES, Chillicothe rocker-stamped, dentate-rocked

GENERAL DATA

New subtype not previously described. For further information see Prufer and McKenzie (1965:27-29). Present definition is based upon the following sample obtained from seven sites: Turner (107), Harness (13), Fort Ancient (4), Hopewell (2), Seip (199), Mound City (6), and Marriott-1 (19):

Body sherds,	grit:	284
	limestone:	45
	mixed:	6
Rim sherds,	grit:	14
	limestone:	1
		350

PASTE

Method of manufacture: Coiled.

Temper: Fine to medium grit or limestone. Particle density is variable, but generally medium. Variability in both size and density has to some extent—but not exclusively—a pattern that appears related to the chronological position of the sites. Thus, at Seip, which in general yielded the qualitatively best sherds of the Hopewellian series, these factors are markedly on the fine side. This is also true of Harness, but here the sample is rather limited. On the other hand, at sites like Turner, which are considered late within the Hopewellian Phase, the emphasis is on coarser particles, and a denser particle distribution, though finer sherds are not entirely lacking.

Texture: Within the framework of the type itself (Prufer and McKenzie, 1965:27-29), the same pattern as that outlined under temper prevails: the best series of sherds was found at Seip.

Hardness: No measurements taken (see Prufer and McKenzie, 1965: 18). The above observations on variability prevail.

Color: Same as for the type in general (Prufer and McKenzie, 1965: 27-29).

SURFACE TREATMENT

Dentate rocker-stamping, zoned or unzoned, covers the entire body with the exception of neck and base. The sample includes 74 zoned sherds. The boundary between neck and body usually consists of a broad incised line. Rocker-stamping ranges from carefully executed to moderately "wild," the quantitative variability of these qualitative elements following the same, apparently chronologically significant pattern as outlined above. Seip, again, has the best decorations.

The length of the rocker swings ranges from short (10 to 15 mm) to very long (up to 50 mm), but this does not seem to carry any particular significance; it occurs at all sites with adequate samples.

Within the stamping a variety of forms, apparently reflecting different stamping tools, can be distinguished.

Variant *A*: Stamps with very fine dentations; usually short, which tend to be dragged from impression to impression.

Variant *B*: Stamps of medium length with distinct, well-spaced, square or rectangular dentations. They are rarely, if ever, dragged.

Variant *C*: Long stamps with huge square or rectangular dentations which are widely spaced. During application the ends of these stamps were firmly and deeply planted into the clay. When this kind of stamping was smoothed—as it often was—these deep impressions tend to show up as pseudopunctations. Occasionally this variety of stamping carried on to the base.

Smoothing of various degrees occurs on many sherds, though it is heavy and predominant only on stamping style *C*.

The distribution of stamping styles *A* and *C* is predominantly, but not exclusively, restricted to Seip. Style *B* occurs everywhere. For further data see the discussion of Seip ceramics.

The zones, where they occur, range from extremely well executed, angular, or curvilinear at Seip, to shoddy and carelessly executed at such sites as Turner. In the case of the carefully zoned sherds the zones are broad (2 to 3 mm) incisions; in the poorly executed examples they are narrow incisions.

At Seip most sherds have moderate to fine exterior surface polish. At late sites, such as Turner, this is nearly absent, though one vessel from the Turner cemetery area (Pl. 30) conforms to the highest standards.

Rim decorations include cross-hatching above a punctate band, as well as vertical- or horizontal-dentate rocker-stamping. The quality of these decorations corresponds to that of the body decorations.

FORM

Rim: This ranges from typical thickened or unthickened Hopewell Rims, to straight-vertical, and straight-flaring. The best classic examples occur at Seip, where straight-vertical and straight-flaring rims are very rare. At Turner all forms occur, but the straight rims predominate, showing great size variability.

Lip: Lips are flattened or slightly rounded.

Body: Body forms are variable. Included are cylindrical straight-sided vessels, elongated (quasi-cylindrical) semiglobular vessels, and globular ones. Occasionally lobing occurs. Size ranges from small to large, with the small to medium range predominating, at all but the late sites, where large vessels seem to have been the rule.

Base: Bases are flat (in the case of cylindrical vessels) and rounded.

Thickness: Body sherds: *Circa* 85 per cent of the sample was measured:

Range:	3-10 mm
Mean:	4.4 mm

Rim sherds: All measurable rims were measured:

Range:	4-8 mm
Mean:	5.8 mm

Appendages: None.

GEOGRAPHICAL RANGE

While not present at all sites, this subtype occurs throughout the Hopewellian area of southern Ohio.

CHRONOLOGICAL POSITION

Through the entire middle and late range of the Ohio Hopewellian Phase.

PROBABLE RELATIONSHIPS

The Hopewellian Series in general, and the Chillicothe Rocker-stamped type in particular, are the most obvious relatives of this subtype. Farther afield, this subtype and its local relatives are connected with the equivalent types of other areas, notably Illinois.

There remain to be discussed those untyped sherds which have produced more than twelve specimens distributed at more than one site. Their basic characteristics and possible affiliations will here be briefly summarized. Untyped groups with more than twelve sherds, but occurring at a single site only—such as the platters from Seip—should be looked up in the discussion section for the particular mounds or sites in which they occurred.

HOPEWELLIAN SERIES, Untyped Zoned

Ohio Hopewell sites have produced a total of 51 such sherds: Turner (11), Harness (17), Hopewell (5), Fort Ancient (3), Seip (7), Mound City (6), and McGraw (2). Their distribution is as follows:

Body sherds, grit:	39
limestone:	5
mixed:	6
Rim sherds, limestone:	1
	51

Metric attributes show a range of 3 to 9 mm, and a mean of 4.3 mm for body sherds. The single rim is 5 mm thick and cross-hatched. Body decorations consist of incised zones; the incisions are usually about 2 to 3 mm wide. These sherds are similar to the Illinoian type Hopewell Zoned Incised (Griffin, 1952:118). Vessel size ranges from medium to large; vessels appear to have been globular.

SOUTHEASTERN SERIES, Untyped Diamond Check-stamped

The following Ohio sites yielded a total of 22 such sherds: Harness (13), Seip (8), and Rockhold (1). The distribution is as follows:

Body sherds, grit:	12
sandy grit:	1
Rim sherds, sand:	8
grit:	1
	22

The body sherds have a thickness range of 4 to 10 mm, with a mean of 7.5 mm. Mean rim thickness is 8.5 mm. These very thick sherds (with a single exception from Harness) are decorated with large diamond check-stamping which has in all cases been smoothed over to the point of near-elimination. The vessels appear to have been very large and quasi-cylindrical, with straight, near-vertical rims and, probably flat bases.

SOUTHEASTERN SERIES, Untyped Cord-marked

The following sites have yielded a total of 45 sherds which have been grouped under this heading: Turner (17), Fort Ancient (14), McGraw (9), Harness (2), Russell Brown (1), Seip (1), and Marriott-1 (1). Included here are sherds of all temper attributes, if they have tetrapodal supports, and general body sherds that are sand tempered. The distribution is as follows:

Body sherds, sand:		16
Tetrapods, grit:		23
	limestone:	4
	sand:	1
		44

Metric data on thickness were taken for the body sherds only; the range is 5 to 8 mm, with a mean of 6.1 mm. The affiliations of this material remain to be established.

SOUTHEASTERN SERIES, Untyped Complicated-stamped

The following sites have yielded a total of 13 complicated-stamped sherds: Seip (11), and Turner (2). In addition, such sherds were recovered from the Boone Rockshelter in Jackson County, Ohio (Mills, 1912: Fig. 6); these sherds are not included here, because their provenience is very poorly documented. The distribution is as follows:

Body sherds, grit:		1
	limestone:	2
	sand:	8
		11

The thickness range for these sherds is 5 to 9 mm, with a mean of 5.9 mm. Many of the sherds from Seip are black. It is obvious that this material is not indigenous to Ohio.

SOUTHEASTERN SERIES, Untyped Plain

The following sites have yielded a total of 97 sherds which are here grouped under the above heading: Turner (28), McGraw (15), Rockhold (4), Seip (3), Hopewell (2), Fort Hill (1), Marriott-1 (1), and Russell Brown (43). The criteria for this classification were the presence of sand temper and/or tetrapodal supports on otherwise undecorated sherds. A difficulty that arises here is that it can be demonstrated that a number of simple-stamped vessels are plain above the body; furthermore, some of the tetrapodal supports may also have been part of decorated vessels. The sherds in some cases are not large enough to determine this. Thus, the classification here may not be entirely reliable. Sherd distribution is as follows:

Body sherds, sand:		46
Rim sherds, sand:		8
Tetrapods,	grit:	33
	limestone:	7
	sand:	3
		97

No metric data were taken for tetrapods. The range of thickness for body sherds is 4 to 8 mm with a mean of 4.7 mm. The range of rim thickness is 3 to 5 mm with a mean of 3.8 mm. The vessels, with one round-based exception from Turner, appear to be all tetrapodal. In shape they seem to have been globular and rather small. Most of the extant rims—if indeed they belong here—are similar to the everted rims of simple-stamped vessels. The exception consists of two rims resembling Hopewell Rims from Russell Brown-2; these clearly belong to plain vessels.

IV

SITES

HARNESS

The Harness Group of earthworks and mounds was excavated on four different occasions. The first exploration, by Squier and Davis (1848), provides no clues as to ceramics from the site which then was known as the Liberty Earthworks. A more detailed report is available on the excavations carried out by F. W. Putnam for the Peabody Museum of Harvard University. (Putnam, 1886: 404-07). Putnam excavated five of the component mounds of the group, partly including the large Edwin Harness Mound. It is stated in the brief published report on these operations that one of the structures, a mound north of the great earthwork circle yielded " . . . a large bed of ashes and charcoal about at the level of the natural surface upon which the mound was made. This ash bed covered nearly the whole area occupied by the mound, and in it we found many fragments of pottery . . . . Near the centre of the mound, extending to the south, was a long narrow pit, about 9 × 2 feet, which was a foot in depth. At the bottom of this pit were burnt bones" (Putnam, 1886*a*:405). In the Peabody Museum collections and catalogue this mound is referred to as "Mound-4." The ceramics are catalogued under numbers 35121-35133. Though it is clear from the catalogue references in the Peabody Museum that at least one other mound, "Mound-3," yielded pottery, this is not mentioned in Putnam's report, but the catalogue references (Nos. 35078-79) indicate that pottery was found. Putnam's excavations in the Edwin Harness Mound produced only two sherds which are catalogued under numbers 34947 and 34960.

It should be noted here, that Harness-3 and Harness-4 are part of a group of mounds outside the earthworks; in 1961 Frank Soday dug in several of the other structures here, which he named Russell Brown Mounds (see discussion under this name). It is of extreme importance to note that the peculiar biglobular bird vessel found by Putnam in Harness-4 can be duplicated by two further such vessels found by Soday in one of the Brown Mounds.

In 1896 Moorehead (1897) excavated parts of the large Edwin Harness Mound in a manner that should be a warning to all neophyte archaeologists; he tunnelled through the structure like a rodent, with both eyes firmly glued on the loot that this tumulous might (and did) yield. There is no reference to pottery in Moorehead's report on this enterprise. The final excavation of this large structure was conducted by Mills for the Ohio Historical Society in 1930. In his report, Mills offers a brief discussion on the ceramics (Mills, 1907:158-62) from this mound, noting that "... in every part of the mound fragments of broken pottery, representing a high type of fictile art were found." The only specific reference to location within the mound is the sad statement that "... a perfect piece had been placed upon the clay covering of one of the uncremated dead about eighteen inches above the body, and was accidentally broken by being struck with a digging tool by one of the workmen, and the vase shattered, but we hope to be able to restore it" (Mills, 1907:160). If this vessel is still in existence, I have not been able to trace it in the collections of the Ohio State Museum, where both Moorehead's and Mills' collections are stored under catalogue number 7/100.

The material in the Peabody Museum consists of 294 sherds; that in the Ohio State Museum of 177 sherds.

Analysis: Harness-3

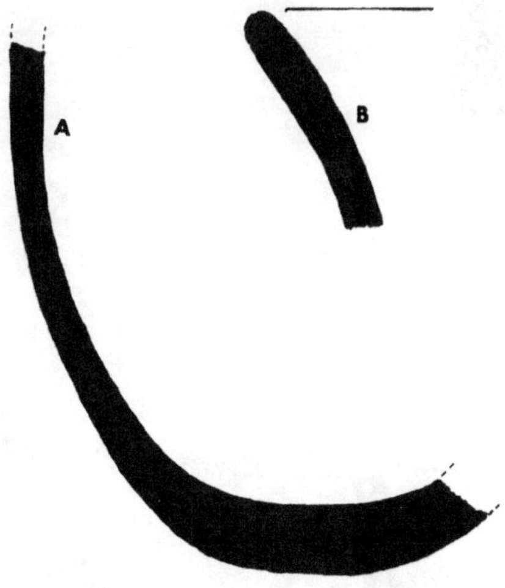

Fig. 1. Harness-3. (A) Chillicothe Rocker-stamped, plain-rocked; (B) McGraw Plain.

Scioto Series, McGraw Plain—47 (Fig. 1, B)
Body sherds, Grit: 45 (4-5 mm; 4.5 mm)
Rim sherds, Grit: 2 (5.0 mm)

Hopewellian Series, Chillicothe Rocker-stamped—1 (Fig. 1, A)
A. Plain-rocked: 1
Body sherds, Grit: 1 (body: 4 mm; base 6 mm)

Comments

The Hopewellian Series vessels had round bases. The distribution of the various ceramic series from Harness-3 is as follows:

	Percent	Sherds
Scioto Series:	97.91	47
Hopewellian Series:	2.08	1

Within the Scioto Series only McGraw Plain sherds were found, i.e. N = 100 per cent. Since all sherds are grit tempered, N = 100 per cent.

Analysis: Harness-4

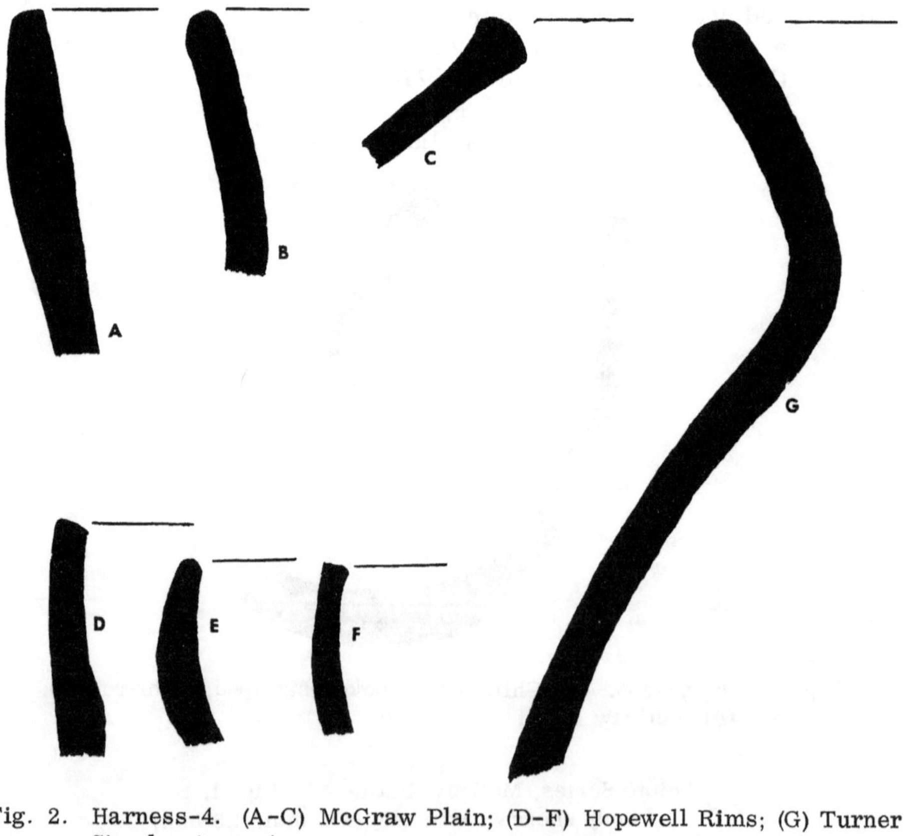

Fig. 2. Harness-4. (A-C) McGraw Plain; (D-F) Hopewell Rims; (G) Turner Simple-stamp *A*.

Scioto Series, McGraw Cord-marked—85 (Pl. 1*a*)
Body sherds, Grit: 79 (3- 7 mm; 5.4 mm)
Clay: 6 (3- 7 mm; 5.5 mm)

Scioto Series, McGraw Plain—38 (Fig. 2, A-C)
Body sherds, Grit: 28 (3-13 mm; 7.0 mm)
Rim sherds, Grit: 10 (5- 8 mm; 6.5 mm)

Hopewellian Series, Chillicothe Rocker-stamped—23 (Pl. 1*b*)
A. Plain-rocked: 21
Body sherds, Grit: 21 (--)*
(zoned: 14)
D. Dentate-rocked: 2
Body sherds, Grit: 2 (--)*
(zoned: 2)

Hopewellian Series, Seip Plain—2
Body sherds, Grit: 2 (--)*
(lobed: 1)

Hopewellian Series, Untyped Zoned Incised—16 (Pl. 1*c*)
Body sherds, Grit: 16 (--)*

Hopewellian Series, Biglobular (bird) Vessel—1 (Pl. 2)
1/2 vessel, Grit: 1 (4- 5 mm)

Hopewellian Series, Hopewell Rims—5 (Fig. 2, D-F)
Grit: 5 (4- 5 mm; 4.4 mm)

Southeastern Series, Turner Simple-stamped *A*—62 (Fig. 2, G)
Body sherds, Grit: 59 (mean only: 5.0 mm)
Rim sherds, Grit: 3 (mean only: 5.0 mm)

Southeastern Series, Untyped Diamond Check-stamped—1
Body sherds, Grit: 1 (4 mm)

Unknown Series, Untyped Plain (painted?)—1
Body sherds, Grit: 1 (5 mm)

Total 234 sherds

Comments

With the exception of the biglobular bird vessel and the old painted or filmed sherd discussed below, the pottery from Harness-4 is entirely in line with the typed series. The following points, however, deserve specific mention. In the McGraw Cord-marked series, the clay tempered sherds have uniformly widely-spaced fine-cord impressions. Among the McGraw Plain material two groups of possible significance can be distinguished. The bulk of the sherds (37 body sherds and 9 rims) conforms to the type description. The metric data for body sherds here are 3 to 9 mm;

*Metric data are available only for all Hopewellian Series body sherds: 3 to 7; 5.0 mm.

PLATE 1

Harness-4. (*a*) McGraw Cord-marked; (*b*) Chillicothe Rocker-stamped, plain-rocked; (*c*) Hopewellian Series, Untyped Incised.

PLATE 2

Harness-4. Biglobular Bird Vessel. (Photograph by Peabody Museum, Harvard University.)

mean 4.6 mm. In addition there are 10 body sherds and 1 rim sherd with extremely coarse grit temper. The metric data for body thickness give a range from 12 to 13 mm, with a mean of 12.5 mm. The single rim is thinned and measures 7 mm. One sherd has a large lug, suggestive of certain Adena types.

In the Hopewellian Series the zoned incised sherds are of interest. The zoning is wide and angular. One Hopewell Rim shows marked interior grooving.

The biglobular vessel has been described as follows: It is "... about 6 inches in height .... It is of depressed double globular form. The entire lower section is covered with a design composed of triangles made up of bands three-eights of an inch wide, filled with zigzag markings [fine dentate rocker-stamping]. The upper section is somewhat smaller than the lower, and is ornamented with a zone in which are six highly conventionalized bird figures, the space within the incised outlines of each bird being filled with the usual zigzag pattern. Each alternate bird is reversed" (Willoughby and Hooten, 1922:92). This vessel is in all respects similar to the two specimens from Russell Brown Mound-1. The birds appear to represent the shoveler duck.

In the Southeastern Series, the diamond check-stamped sherd, except for being rather thin, appears to be similar to the specimens of this presumed type from Seip and Rockhold.

The Untyped Plain sherd appears to be red filmed or painted, and shows three "jab and drag" punctations.

The distribution of the various ceramic series from Harness-4 is as follows:

	Percent	Sherds
Scioto Series:	54.50	133
Hopewellian:	19.26	47
Southeastern Series:	25.82	63
Other:	.41	1

Within the Scioto Series (N = 133) the distribution of McGraw Cord-marked and McGraw Plain is as follows:

	Percent	Sherds
McGraw Cord-marked:	63.91	85
McGraw Plain:	36.09	48

The temper distribution for the total series is as follows:

	Percent	Sherds
Grit:	97.54	238
Clay:	2.45	6

Analysis: Edwin Harness Mound

Scioto Series, McGraw Cord-marked—67 (Fig. 3, G; Pl. 3; 4*a, f*)

Body sherds, Grit:		63 (3- 8 mm; 5.1 mm)
	Limestone:	1 (10 mm)
	Shell:	1 (5 mm)
Rim sherds, Grit:		2 (4- 7 mm; 5.5 mm)

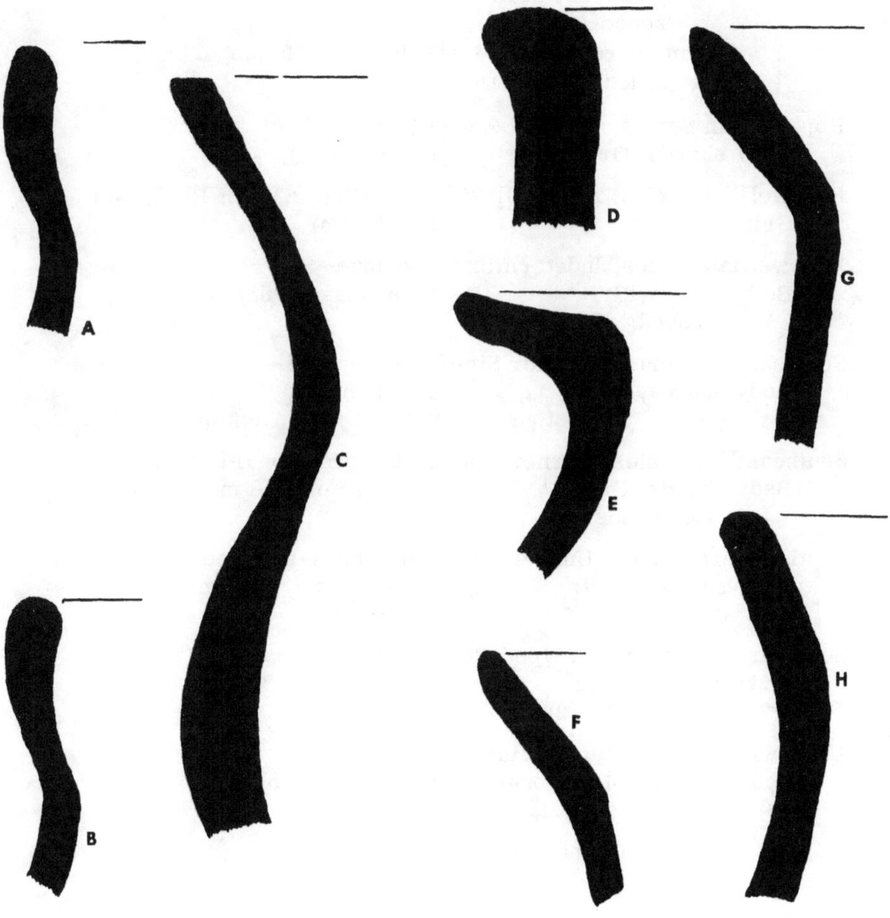

Fig. 3. Edwin Harness. (A-B) Hopewell Rims; (C) Chillicothe Rocker-stamped, dentate-rocked on rim; (D-F, H) McGraw Plain; (G) McGraw Cord-marked.

Scioto Series, McGraw Plain—28 (Fig. 3, D-F, H)
Body sherds, Grit: 16 (3- 9 mm; 5.7 mm)
Rim sherds, Grit: 7 (5-15 mm; 7.5 mm)
Limestone: 4 (6- 8 mm; 6.7 mm)
Shell: 1 (7 mm)

Hopewellian Series, Chillicothe Rocker-stamped—27
A. Plain-rocked: 16 (Pl. 5, *a*)
Body sherds, Grit: 16 (5- 7 mm; 5.5 mm)
(zoned: 3; lobed: 1)
D. Dentate-rocked: 11 (Fig. 3, C)
Body sherds, Grit: 9 (3- 5 mm; 4.2 mm)
(zoned-lobed: 2)
Rim sherds, Grit: 2 (6-10 mm; 8.0 mm)
(zoned-lobed: 1)

Hopewellian Series, Untyped Zoned Incised—1
Body sherds, Grit: 1 (6 mm)

Hopewellian Series, Hopewell Rims—4 (Fig. 3, A-B; Pl. 5, *b-c*)
Grit: 4 (8.0 mm)

Hopewellian Series, Indeterminate Residue—5
Body sherds, Grit: 5 (unmeasurable)
(zoned: 2)

Southeastern Series, Turner Simple-stamped *A*—13 (Pl. 4, *b, c, e*)
Body sherds, Grit: 5 (4.0 mm)
Limestone: 8 (6- 8 mm; 7.0 mm)

Southeastern Series, Turner Check-stamped—19 (Pl. 4, *d*)
Body sherds, Grit: 19 (3- 7 mm; 3.8 mm)
(tetrapods: 1)

Southeastern Series, Untyped Diamond Check-stamped-12
Body sherds, Grit: 11 (7- 9 mm; 7.5 mm)
Rim sherds, Grit: 1 (9 mm)

Southeastern Series, Untyped Cord-marked—2
Body sherds, Grit: 2 (--)
(tetrapods: 2)

Unknown Series, Untyped Widely-incised
Body sherds, Limestone: 1 (unmeasurable)

Total 179 sherds
Grand Total 461 sherds

Comments

For the Scioto Series only the two shell-tempered sherds deserve special notice. Both specimens are clearly part of this

PLATE 3

Edwin Harness. McGraw Cord-marked.

PLATE 4

Edwin Harness. (*a,f*) McGraw Cord-marked; (*b,c,e*) Turner Simple-stamped *A*; (*d*) Turner Check-stamped.

PLATE 5

Edwin Harness. (*a*) Chillicothe Rocker-stamped, plain-rocked; (*b*,*c*) Hopewell Rims.

series, that is, they are not intrusive. The shell temper particles are small and of low density in the sherd body. I suggest that they simply represent a local, erratic substitute for the usual tempering materials, in this case perhaps limestone.

In the Hopewellian Series large vessels predominate. The decorations are boldly executed, and show no indications of pattern dissolution. Slight to moderate polishing is common on most sherds.

The diamond check-stamped sherds are thick-bodied, the stamping is large, and as in the case of this material from other sites, the stamping has been nearly eliminated by smoothing. The untyped incised sherd is too small for definition; the incisions are deep and wide.

The distribution of the various ceramic series from the Edwin Harness Mound is as follows:

	Percent	Sherds
Scioto Series:	53.07	95
Hopewellian Series:	20.67	37
Southeastern Series:	25.69	46
Other:	.56	1

Within the Scioto Series (N = 95) the distribution of McGraw Cord-marked and McGraw Plain is as follows:

	Percent	Sherds
McGraw Cord-marked:	70.52	67
McGraw Plain:	29.47	28

The temper distribution for the total series is as follows:

	Percent	Sherds
Grit:	91.07	163
Limestone:	7.82	14
Shell:	1.11	2

The discrepancies between Griffin's analysis (1945) and the present results need not be of much concern. First, Griffin apparently did not include the Peabody collections in his work and, second, he does not seem to have had access to all of the sherds in the Ohio State Museum, because he states that in the sample from that institution, "There are no sand tempered sherds or simple stamping of any kind" (1945:241). While the former statement is correct, the latter is not.

ROCKHOLD

This group of two classic Hopewell mounds in Ross County, Ohio, was excavated *circa* 35 years ago by the Ohio Historical Society. Beyond a casual notice (Greenman, 1930), the rich contents of these tumuli have never been published. No specific provenience data on the ceramics are available beyond mound attribution. The material is deposited in the Ohio State Museum under catalogue number 1020.

Analysis: Rockhold-1

Southeastern Series, Untyped Diamond check-stamped—1 (Fig. 4, A)
Vessel, Sandy Grit: 1 (rim: 8 mm; body: 10 mm)

Comments

This represents a substantial part of a very large thick vessel with diamond check-stamping. The stamping is almost completely obliterated by smoothing. The fabric is thick and extremely crumbly. Undoubtedly much of the tempering material is sand, though there is also a considerable amount of crushed rock. For purposes of precise classification this is called sand temper. The color is grey. Similar sherds have also been reported from Seip and Harness.

Analysis: Rockhold-2

Scioto Series, McGraw Cord-marked—51

Body sherds, Grit:	50	(3-11 mm; 6.5 mm)
Rim sherds, Grit:	1	(9 mm)

Scioto Series, McGraw Plain—42

Body sherds, Grit:	39	(4-11 mm; 6.9 mm)
Rim sherds, Grit:	3	(5- 7 mm; 6.0 mm)

Hopewellian Series, Brangenberg Plain—1

Rim sherds, Grit:	1	(10 mm)

Southeastern Series, Turner Simple-stamped *A*—1

Body sherds, Grit:	1	(6 mm)

Southeastern Series, Untyped Plain—4

Body sherds,	Grit:	1	(--)
(tetrapodal)	Sand:	2	(3- 4 mm; 3.5 mm)
Rim sherds,	Sand:	1	(3 mm)

Miami Series, Cord-wrapped stick stamped on rim—1 (Fig. 4, B)
Rim sherds, Clay: 1 (unmeasurable; split)

Total 100 sherds
Grand Total 101 sherds

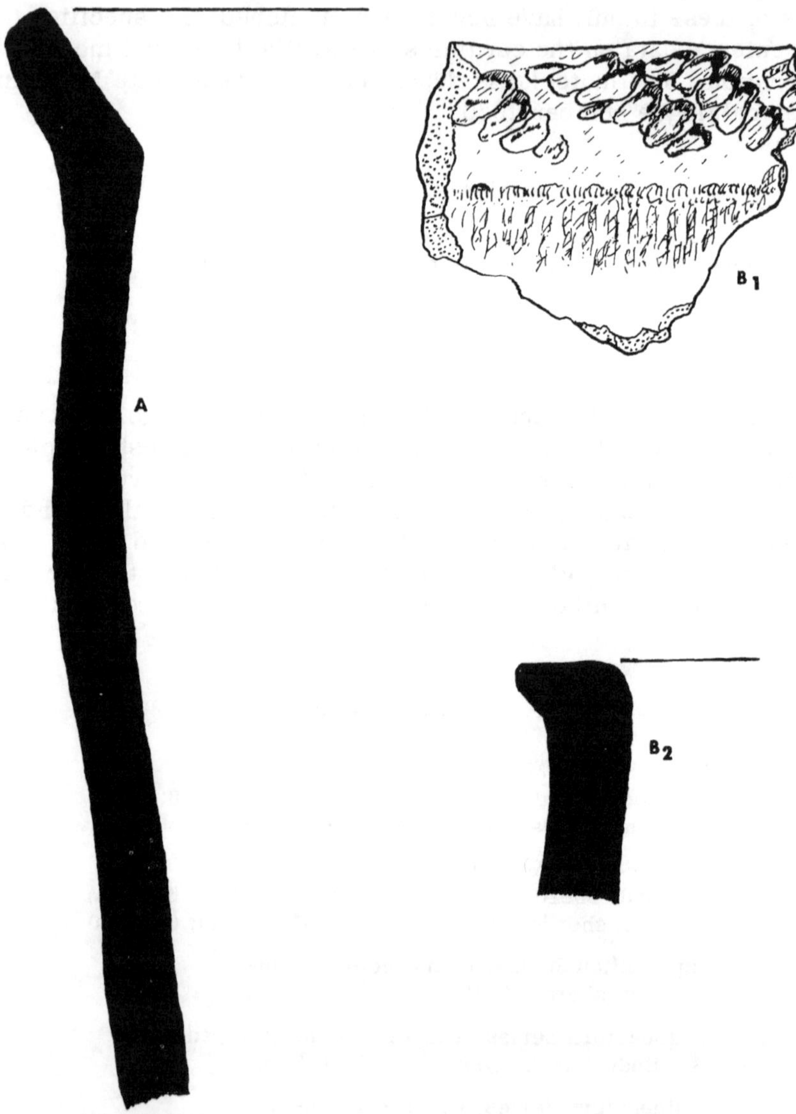

Fig. 4. Rockhold-1. (A) Southeastern Series, Untyped Diamond check-stamped. Rockhold-2. (B) Miami Series, Cord-wrapped Stick on Rim.

Comments

The Untyped Plain sherds of the Southeastern Series are similar to Turner Simple-stamped *A* and *B* as far as fabrics and vessel morphology are concerned. The single sherd of the Miami Series has a cord-marked body; the rim treatment is identical with that of certain Weaver vessels in Illinois illustrated by Griffin (1952: Pl. 37, *c*).

The distribution of the various ceramic series from Rockhold-2 is as follows:

	Percent	Sherds
Scioto Series:	93.00	93
Hopewellian Series:	1.00	1
Southeastern Series:	5.00	5
Miami Series:	1.00	1

Within the Scioto Series (N = 93) the distribution of McGraw Cord-marked and McGraw Plain is as follows:

	Percent	Sherds
McGraw Cord-marked:	54.84	51
McGraw Plain:	45.16	42

The temper distribution for the total series is as follows:

	Percent	Sherds
Grit:	96.00	96
Sand:	4.00	3
Clay:	1.00	1

HOPEWELL

Ceramic data on this classic mound group in Ross County, Ohio, are unusually inadequate. During the past 125 years the thirty-eight mounds of this site have been repeatedly examined. The first survey, entailing some excavations, was undertaken by Squier and Davis (1848). In 1891-92 Warren King Moorehead carried out extensive excavations in several mounds for the World's Columbian Exposition. It is clear from the chapter on ceramics in his site report (1922) that pottery was rare. In the present analysis only the few sherds still extant from Moorehead's "diggings" could be used. They are deposited in the Chicago Natural History Museum and the Ceramic Repository of the

Museum of Anthropology at the University of Michigan. It is my impression that originally there were more sherds, but I was unable to trace them.

The final exploration of the Hopewell group was carried out by Shetrone for the Ohio Historical Society, between 1922 and 1925. There is little point in sifting the voluminous text of Shetrone's site report in order to attempt a correlation between extant sherds in the Ohio State Museum and those referred to in the text: the cataloguing of the ceramic material does not permit this. It is only possible to go by certain illustrated specimens (Shetrone, 1926:127) for which gross provenience data are given. The catalogue number is uniformly given as 283 for all materials from the Hopewell group. On the basis of correlating illustrations with text data, two specific provenience units could be isolated. Shetrone shows a number of sherds (1926:127, Fig. 52) which were recovered from the so-called "auxiliary mounds," numbering 30 to 38. On the same page, Fig. 53 illustrates a series of sherds, the provenience of which was Hopewell-17. In the text it is stated that one of the ceremonial caches in this structure yielded, *inter alia*, pottery. The sherds themselves are still in the collection.

The only other data on pottery which might be of some relevance are contained in a brief section of Shetrone's report (1926: 125-26). Here it is stated that "Occasional pieces of ceremonial vessels were found scattered through the soil or on the floors of the several mounds."

Other data on specific loci stem from Moorehead's earlier work, and from a notation on a sherd in the Ohio State Museum. A fairly complete vessel was found by Moorehead in one of the two small habitation areas between mounds, but within the earthwork enclosure. A second vessel was found in "altar-1" of Mound-25; it belongs with the Hopewellian Series. Apart from its relatively complete condition, this vessel is of significance, because the feature in which it was found has yielded a radiocarbon date of 1 ± 200 B.C. (C-136). A single sherd in the Ohio State Museum came from Hopewell-2.

In summation, then, four specific provenience units can be distinguished for the Hopewell group: Hopewell-17, "altar-1" of Hopewell-25, the "auxiliary mounds," and one of the habitation areas. The remaining material can only be dealt with under the heading of Hopewell-General.

Analysis: Hopewell-2

Southeastern Series, Turner Simple-stamped *A*—1

Body sherds: Limestone: 1 (6 mm)

Analysis: Hopewell-17

Hopewellian Series, Chillicothe Rocker-stamped—4
A. Plain-rocked: 3
Body sherds, Grit: 3 (3- 6 mm; 5.3 mm)
(zoned, 2; lobed: 1)
B. Dentate-rocked: 1
Rim sherd, Grit: 1 (6 mm)
(zoned: 1)

Hopewellian Series, Untyped Zoned Incised—1 (Fig. 5, E)
Body sherds, Grit: 1 (7 mm)

Southeastern Series, Turner Simple-stamped *A*—1
Body sherds, Grit: 1 (body: 5 mm; base: 11 mm)
(tetrapodal)

Total 6 sherds

Comments

The fabrics and decorations of the Hopewellian Series are of fairly good quality, though they do not approach Illinoian standards. The simple-stamped tetrapodal vessel was large.

The distribution of the various ceramic series from Hopewell-17 is as follows:

	Percent	Sherds
Hopewellian Series:	83.33	5
Southeastern Series:	16.66	1

Grit temper being the only material, N = 100 per cent.

Analysis: Hopewell-25 ("Altar-1")

Hopewellian Series, Chillicothe Rocker-stamped—1 (Pl. 6, *a*)
A. Plain-rocked; 1
Vessel, Grit: 1 (body: 6 mm)

Comments

This medium-sized vessel is 22 cms high and 21 cms in diameter at the rim; it has a nearly flat bottom, and is flowerpot-shaped. The body is entirely covered with tight, short, plain rocker-stamping. The rim is thickened and cross-hatched. The cross-hatching is somewhat unusual inasmuch as the hatching occurs in spaced groups. Griffin once thought that the style of

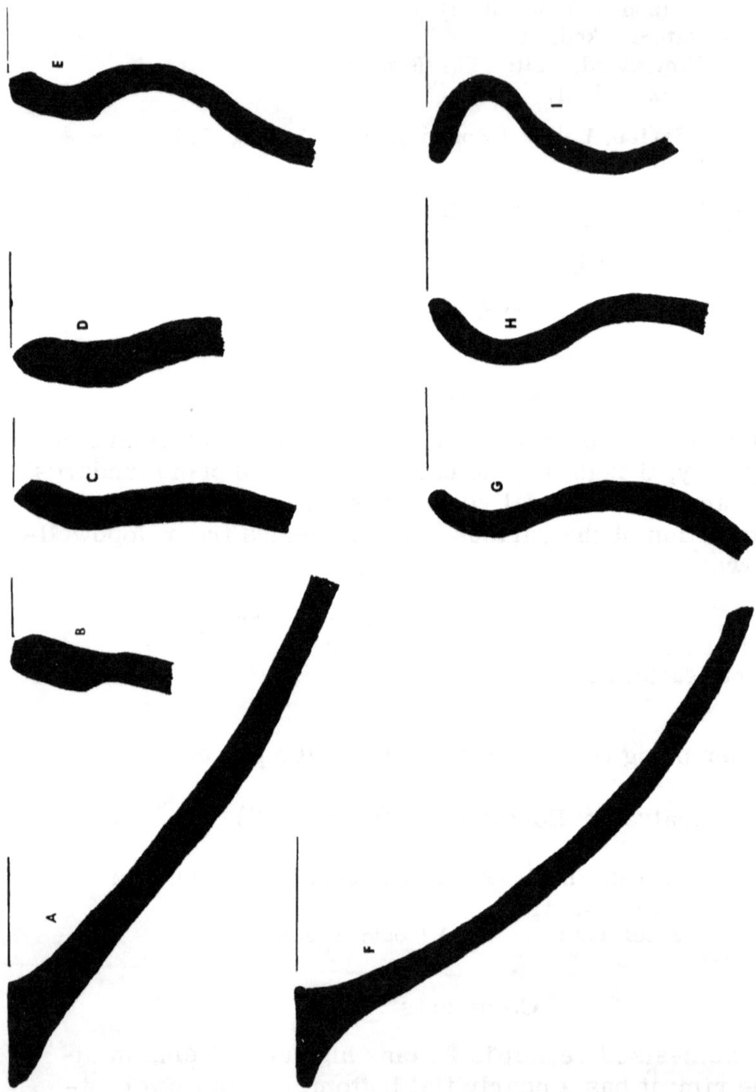

Fig. 5. Hopewell-17. (E) Hopewellian Series, Untyped Zoned Incised. Hopewell Auxiliary Mounds, (F) Brangenberg Plain; (G–I) Seip Plain. Hopewell General. (A) Brangenberg Plain; (B–C) Hopewell Rims; (D) Chillicothe Rocker-stamped, dentate-rocked on rim.

PLATE 6

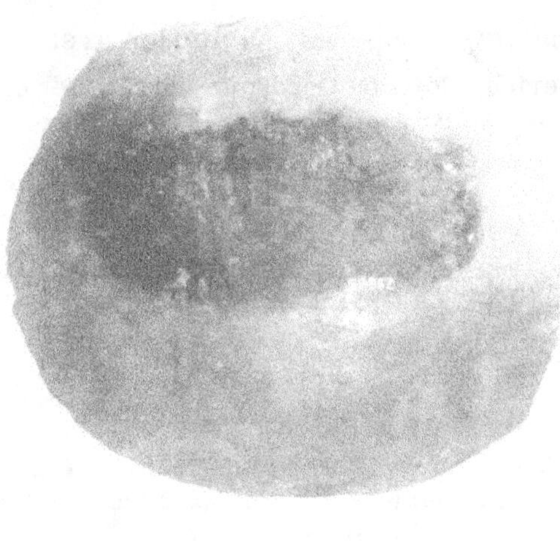

Hopewell-25. (*a*) Chillicothe Rocker-stamped, plain-rocked, Hopewell Habitation Area; (*b*) McGraw Cord-marked, Hopewell General; (*c*) Hopewellian Series, Untyped Black-on-Red Painted. (Figures *a* and *b* photographed at Harvard University, Peabody Museum.)

decoration peculiar to this vessel " . . . is late within the Hopewellian sequence in Illinois" (1958:7). The radiocarbon date, however, argues against this, as well as the decorative evidence from sherds of known late provenience. The decorations are carefully executed.

Analysis: Hopewell- "Auxiliary mounds 30-38"

Hopewellian Series, Seip Plain—4 (Fig. 5, G-I)
Rim sherds, Grit: 4 (5- 6 mm; 5.3 mm)

Hopewellian Series, Brangenberg Plain—1 (Fig. 5, F)
Rim sherds, Grit: 1 (12 mm)

Total 5 sherds

Comments

Fabrics are of good quality, though not quite approaching Illinoian standards or, for that matter, Seip standards. The statistics show that grit temper equals 100 per cent, and that as far as ceramic series are concerned, only the Hopewellian Series is represented in the known sample.

Analysis: Hopewell habitation area

Scioto Series, McGraw Cord-marked—1 (Pl. 6, *b*)
Vessel, Grit: 1 (--)

Comments

This is a small vessel with smoothed cord-marking and a round base. There is a slight shoulder, and moderately constricted neck. The rim is thickened. It measures 14 cms in height, and 13 cms in diameter at the rim.

Analysis: Hopewell-General

Scioto Series, McGraw Cord-marked—316 (Fig. 6, A-F)
Body sherds, Grit: 310 (2-13 mm; 4.9 mm)
Limestone: 1 (7 mm)
Rim sherds, Grit: 5 (4-11 mm; 5.8 mm)

Scioto Series, McGraw Plain—125 (Fig. 6, G-I)
Body sherds, Grit: 105 (3-11 mm; 5.6 mm)
Rim sherds, Grit: 20 (3-14 mm; 5.4 mm)

Hopewellian Series, Chillicothe Rocker-stamped—4
A. Plain-rocked: 3 (Pl. 7, *a*)
Body sherds, Grit: 3 (4- 5 mm; 4.6 mm)
(zoned: 3)

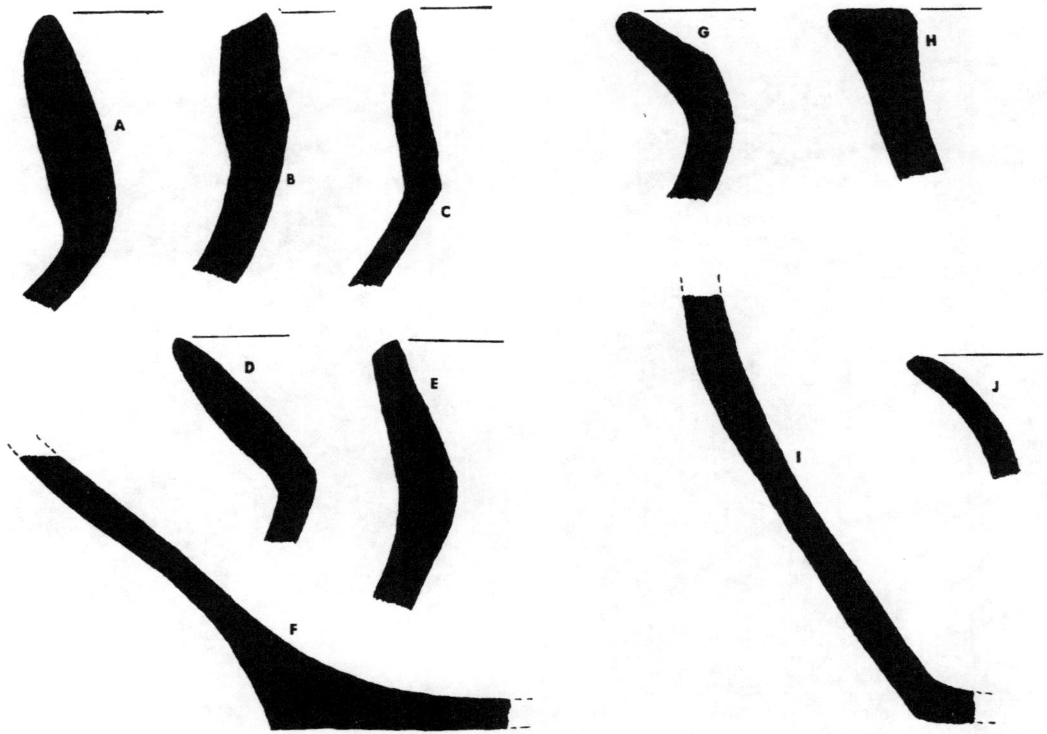

Fig. 6. Hopewell General. (A–F) McGraw Cord-marked; (G–I) McGraw Plain; (J) Southeastern Series, Untyped Plain.

PLATE 7

Hopewell General. (*a*) Chillicothe Rocker-stamped, Plain-rocked; (*b*) Turner Simple-stamped *A*.

D. Dentate-rocked: 1 (Fig. 5, D)
Rim sherds, Grit: 1 (7 mm)
(zoned: 1)

Hopewellian Series, Seip Plain—3
Body sherds, Grit: 2 (5.0 mm)
Rim sherds, Grit: 1 (9 mm)

Hopewellian Series, Brangenberg Plain—1 (Fig. 5, A)
Rim sherds, Grit: 1 (11 mm)

Hopewellian Series, Untyped Zoned Incised—4
Body sherds, Grit: 4 (4- 6 mm; 5.0 mm)

Hopewellian Series, Untyped Black-on-red Painted—1 (Pl. 6, *c*)
Body sherds, Grit: 1 (7 mm)

Hopewellian Series, Hopewell Rims—2 (Fig. 5, B-C)
Grit: 2 (7.0 mm)

Southeastern Series, Turner Simple-stamped *A*—41 (Pl. 7, *b*)
Body sherds, Grit: 40 (4- 6 mm; 4.6 mm)
Limestone: 1 (4 mm)
(tetrapods: 1)

Southeastern Series, Untyped Plain—2 (Fig. 6, J)
Rim sherds, Sand: 2 (3.0 mm)

Total 499 sherds
Grand Total 513 sherds

Comments

The Scioto Series conforms to the type definitions. Hopewellian Series sherds are of relatively good quality, but they neither approach Illinoian standards nor those of Seip in Ohio; on the other hand they are superior in fabrics and decoration to the material from such sites as Turner and McGraw.

The Untyped Zoned Incised sherds appear to represent large vessels; the zoning is deep and rather wide, almost grooved. On the other hand, the Chillicothe Rocker-stamped sherds suggest relatively small vessels. The Untyped Black-on-red Painted sherd is on deposit in the Museum of Anthropology at the University of Michigan (cat. no. 32819). It was excavated by Moorehead (Chicago Natural History Museum, cat. no. 56852). The sherd is grit-tempered; temper particles are very small and of low density within the clay. The fabric is excellent. The sherd bears a shiny polish which overlies the red background color of the vessel as well as the painted black oval areas which seem to have been repeated four times over the vessel. The vessel appears to have been a medium-sized, squat, round pot.

The distribution of the various ceramic series from Hopewell-General is as follows:

	Percent	Sherds
Scioto Series:	88.37	441
Hopewellian Series:	3.00	15
Southeastern Series:	8.61	43

Within the Scioto Series (N = 441) the distribution of McGraw Cord-marked and McGraw Plain is as follows:

	Percent	Sherds
McGraw Cord-marked:	71.65	316
McGraw Plain:	28.34	125

The temper distribution for the total series is as follows:

	Percent	Sherds
Grit:	99.19	495
Limestone:	.40	2
Sand:	.40	2

As far as temper distribution is concerned, the present analysis is in agreement with that by Griffin (1945:241). The discrepancy in the distribution of McGraw Cord-marked (Griffin: 86 per cent; Prufer: 61.79 per cent) and McGraw Plain (Griffin: 10 per cent; Prufer: 24.36 per cent) for the total site collection, can probably be explained by the fact that Griffin had access to additional material from Moorehead's excavations, in the main, apparently from Hopewell-25. That much of this material was cord-marked is indicated by Griffin elsewhere (1958:7). The only major type, however, that does not seem to have been present in the Ohio State Museum collection from Hopewell, but which Moorehead appears to have recovered, consists of some check-stamped sherds (presumably Turner Check-stamped) to which Griffin alludes in his study (1945:241).

ATER

The substantial Ater mound, excavated several years ago by the Ohio Historical Society, remains unpublished. The content of the structure conformed to classic Hopewell standards. Ceramics consisted of a mass of cord-marked sherds, perhaps representing no more than five vessels, found on the floor of the mound. Most of the sherds were very small; the count is restricted to fragments in excess of one centimeter square in size. None of the rims were sufficiently sizeable to warrant illustration. The material is deposited in the Ohio State Museum under catalogue number 3062.

Analysis

Scioto Series, McGraw Cord-marked—505		
Body sherds, Grit:	497	(5-10 mm; 7.3 mm)
Rim sherds, Grit:	8	(5-10 mm; 8.2 mm)

Comments

While the sherds from Ater conform in all major respects to the type definition of McGraw Cord-marked, they seem to be unusually crumbly and poorly fired.

GINTHER

Shetrone, who in 1922 excavated the Ginther platform mound in Ross County, Ohio, has made the following observations on the ceramics from this site, and on their provenience within the structure. Just east of the center of the mound an artificial depression was encountered in the floor. "This was rectangular in form, measuring three feet by five feet, and extended almost east and west. The floor around this basin or depression was heavily covered with coarse sand and fine gravel, of a reddish-yellow color. The pit itself which, when cleared out, was found to be 16 inches in depth, contained, first, a stratum of the same sand as that covering the floor, three inches thick; beneath this, a layer of dark organic matter, interspersed with numerous animal and bird bones, broken pottery-ware, bits of mica, flint chips and mussel shells; below this was a layer, four inches thick, of clayey loam, intermixed with which were a few animal bones; while at the bottom a stratum four inches in thickness was composed of carbonaceous material, containing the same sort of debris as the above strata. Near this pit were two small post-holes" (Shetrone, 1925:159-60).

Northeast of this depression or basin was noted the "... occurrence ... of a post-hole, around which had been laid, covering a rectangular space 11 by 16 inches in extent, carefully fitted fragments of pottery-ware. These, pavement-like in their disposition, were sherds from utility ware, cord-marked, ranging in size from small fragments to pieces three or four inches across" (Shetrone, 1925:160).

A number of features and artifacts, similar in nature to those found above the carefully prepared mound floor, were located beneath this floor. Shetrone adds that among the subfloor features one " . . . appears to have been a food offering, or at least a cache deposit of food. A pit, three feet across, had been dug to a depth of 18 inches below the floor line, and on the flat bottom of this had been deposited a half-bushel of hickory-nuts, of the common shell-bark variety. Around the edges of this deposit were placed, with apparent order, a number of mussel-shells, presumably to serve as spoons or ladles. On top of this deposit, at its center, was the remains of a burned clay vessel, of the utility type, containing a number of animal bones, among which were identified the vertebrae, shoulder-blade and split leg-bones of the deer. Around the pit containing the deposit had been set small posts and stakes, enclosure-like" (Shetrone, 1925:161).

No other information on the pottery from Ginther has appeared in print, nor does the catalogue of the Ohio State Museum provide additional data; the catalogue numbers are 281 and 281/4. From Shetrone's observations it seems apparent that none of the sherds were found in the fill, though it is possible that the material from the submound deposit somewhat predates the construction of the mound. Here on the other hand, the ceramics do not, on typological grounds, suggest any temporal differences.

Analysis

Scioto Series, McGraw Cord-marked—241 (Fig. 7, E-F, Pl. 8, *a-c*)

Body sherds,	Grit:	237	(2- 9 mm; 5.0 mm)
	Limestone:	2	(5.0 mm)
Rim sherds,	Grit:	2	(4.0 mm)

Scioto Series, McGraw Plain—24 (Fig. 7, A-D)

Body sherds,	Grit:	13	(4-11 mm; 5.8 mm)
	Limestone:	2	(5- 6 mm; 5.5 mm)
Rim sherds,	Grit:	9	(5- 7 mm; 5.5 mm)

Southeastern Series, Turner Simple-stamped *B*—6 (Fig. 7, G; Pl. 8, *d-e*)

Body sherds,	Sand:	6	(4.0 mm)
(2 tetrapods)			

Total 271 sherds

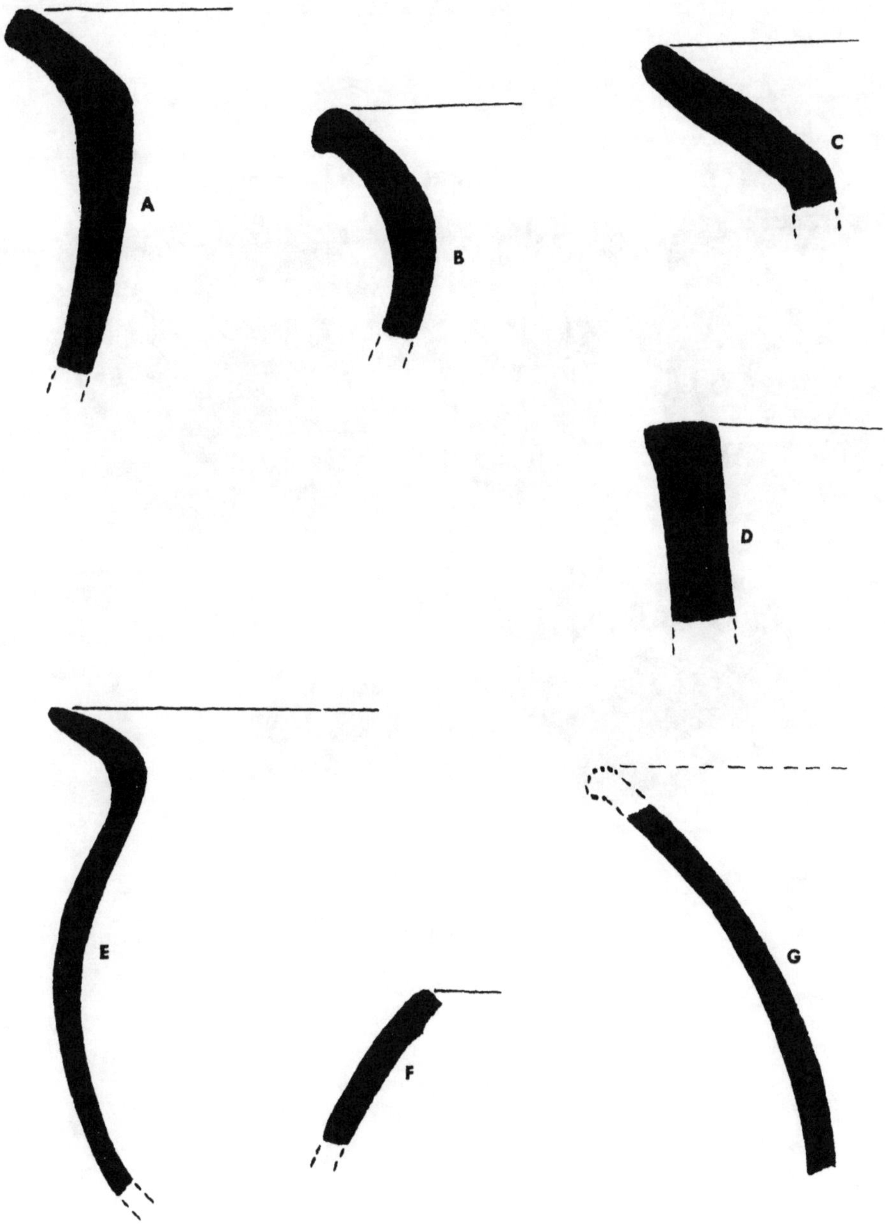

Fig. 7. Ginther. (A-D) McGraw Plain; (E-F) McGraw Cord-marked; (G) Turner Simple-stamped *B*.

PLATE 8

Ginther. (*a–c*) McGraw Cord-marked; (*d–e*) Turner Simple-stamped *B*.

Comments

The ceramics from Ginther conform in all respects to the type definitions. The distribution of the various ceramic series is as follows:

	Percent	Sherds
Scioto Series:	97.78	265
Southeastern Series:	2.21	6

Within the Scioto Series (N = 265) the distribution of McGraw Cord-marked and McGraw Plain is as follows:

	Percent	Sherds
McGraw Cord-marked:	90.94	241
McGraw Plain:	9.05	24

The temper distribution within the total series is as follows:

	Percent	Sherds
Grit:	96.31	261
Limestone:	1.47	4
Sand:	2.21	6

TREMPER

The Tremper mound is located in Scioto County, Ohio; it was excavated by Mills in 1915 for the Ohio Historical Society. Discussions on ceramics in the site report are restricted to the following comments: "The use of pottery by the Tremper mound peoples is certain, as many fragments were found on the floor of the mound . . . only a few pieces of pottery showed design or decoration, the majority of the vessels represented being of the plain type" (Mills, 1916:392-94). In one of the smaller rooms on the north side of the main submound structure " . . . appears to have been a veritable workshop and kitchen, the floor being strewn with the bones of animals, such as the deer, elk, bear, turkey and raccoon. None of these bones had been worked, but all were broken, indicating the use of animals as food. Broken pottery, apparently associated with the preparation and storing of food, was also abundant on this floor . . . " (Mills, 1916:276). The Tremper ceramics are deposited in the Ohio State Museum under catalogue number 125.

Analysis

Scioto Series, McGraw Cord-marked—4 (Fig. 9, C; Pl. 9 *f*)
  Body sherds, Grit: 2 (5- 6 mm; 5.3 mm)
  Rim sherds, Grit: 2 (5.0 mm)

Scioto Series, McGraw Plain—416 (Fig. 9, A, D; Fig. 8, A-I)
  Body sherds, Grit: 207 (3- 9 mm; 5.3 mm)
  Limestone: 188 (3- 8 mm; 4.5 mm)
  Rim sherds, Grit: 20 (4- 8 mm; 5.4 mm)
  Limestone: 1 (10 mm)

Southeastern Series, Turner Simple-stamped *A*—3 (Pl. 9, *a-c*)
  Body sherds, Grit: 3 (6- 9 mm; 7.2 mm)

Southeastern Series, Turner Simple-stamped *B*—3 (Fig. 9, B; Pl. 9,*d-e*)
  Body sherds, Sand: 2 (3.0 mm)
  Rim sherds, Sand: 1 (3 mm)

Unknown Series, Untyped Incised—5 (Pl. 10, *a-c*)
  Body sherds, Clay: 4 (4.0 mm)
  Rim sherds, Clay: 1 (4 mm)

Total 431 sherds

Comments

All typed sherds conform to the type definitions. About half-a-dozen plain sherds may be examples of very finely tempered and polished, thin Seip Plain ware of the Hopewellian Series; in the absence of rims, and in the absence of any other sherds of the Hopewellian Series at Tremper, this can, however, not be ascertained; hence these sherds are submerged in the McGraw Plain group.

The clay tempered, incised sherds are completely atypical of any known Ohio Hopewell affiliated ceramic series. They are soft and crumbly. The color is light yellow-buff. The incisions are shoddily executed.

The distribution of the various ceramic series is as follows:

	Percent	Sherds
Scioto Series:	97.44	420
Southeastern Series:	1.39	6
Other:	1.16	5

Within the Scioto Series (N = 420) the distribution of McGraw Cord-marked and McGraw Plain is as follows:

	Percent	Sherds
McGraw Cord-marked:	.95	4
McGraw Plain:	99.04	416

Fig. 8. Tremper. (A–I) McGraw Plain.

PLATE 9

Tremper. (*a–c*) Turner Simple-stamped *A*; (*d–e*) Turner Simple-stamped *B*; (*f*) McGraw Cord-marked.

PLATE 10

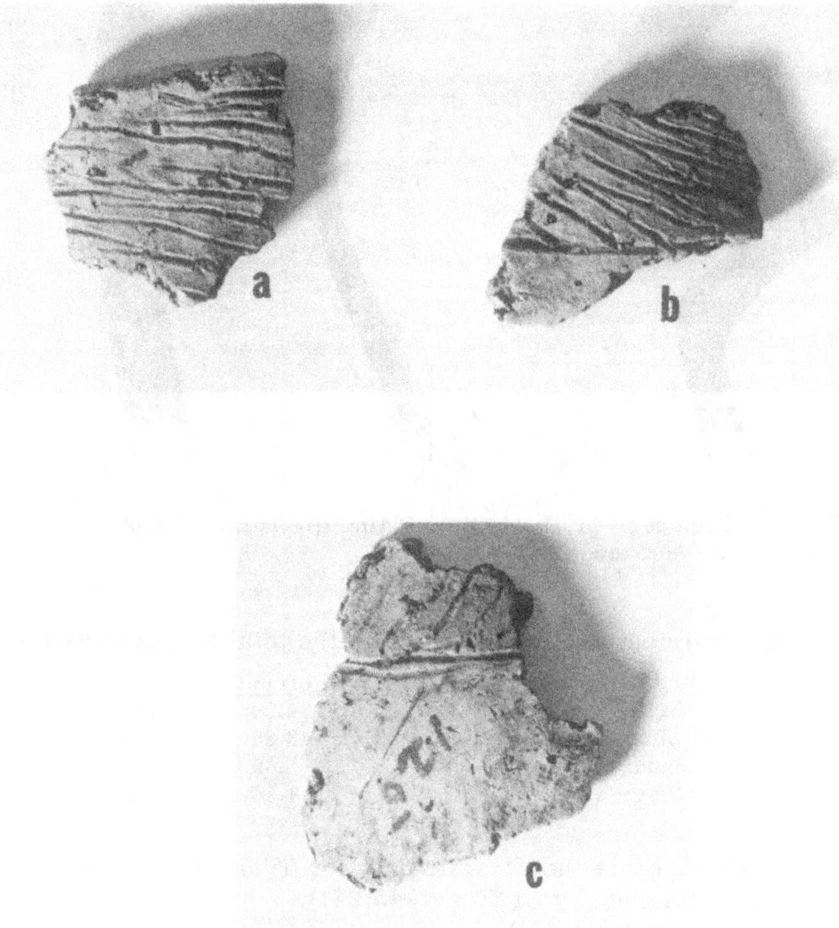

Tremper. (*a–c*) Unknown Series, Untyped Incised.

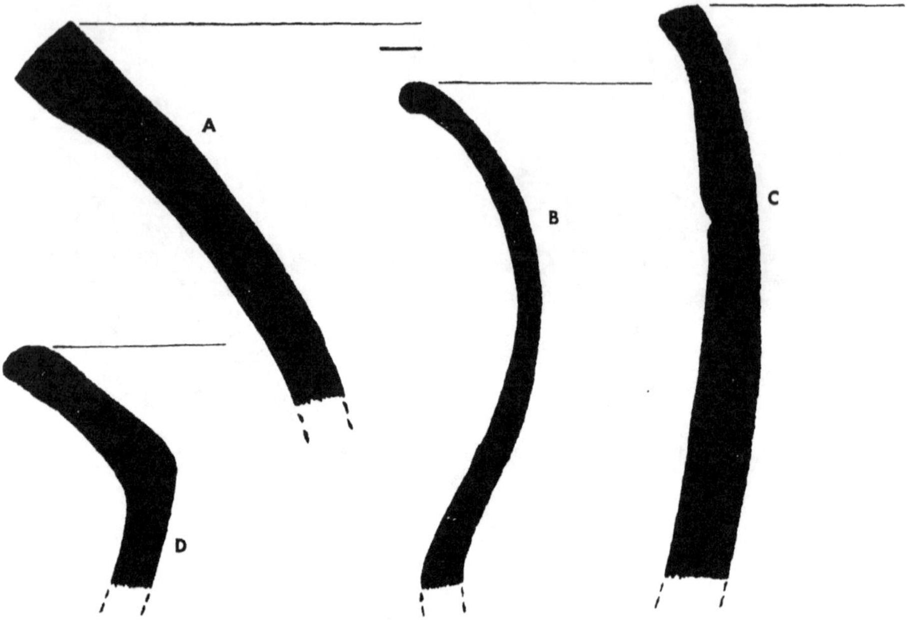

Fig. 9. Tremper. (A, D) McGraw Plain; (B) Turner Simple-stamped *B*; (C) McGraw Cord-marked.

The distribution of temper within the total series is as follows:

	Percent	Sherds
Grit:	54.29	234
Limestone:	43.85	189
Sand:	.69	3
Clay:	1.16	5

In all respects the ceramic data for Tremper seem to agree with those obtained by Griffin (1945:241).

MOUND CITY

The Mound City group in Ross County, Ohio, was first excavated in the early nineteenth century by Squier and Davis (1848). During their explorations ceramics were found, especially in mounds 2 and 3. The only illustrations available of these finds are those of two vessels discovered in the aforementioned structures (Squier and Davis, 1848, Pl. XLVII, 1 and 2).

During World War I Mound City became an army camp (Camp Sherman). Much of the original site was disturbed during this phase of the earthwork's history. After the war, Mills carried out extensive excavations at a number of mounds comprising the group (Mills, 1922). The ceramic data in the present analysis are mainly derived from Mills' collections.

Since 1963 further excavations have been undertaken at the site (Baby and Brown, 1964). A fair amount of pottery was obtained during these operations, but they are not included in this analysis.

The sherds recovered by Mills are deposited in the Ohio State Museum under the catalogue number 260. Since the available records do not permit detailed attribution of sherds to specific provenience units or even mounds, it is, with certain exceptions, unnecessary to quote Mills' report on the site *in extenso.* The report devotes a few pages to a brief discussion of pottery (Mills, 1922:509-13). From this it transpires that two vessels which proved restorable, can be assigned to specific locations. The first is a tetrapodal pot with a bird design which was found in Mound City-2, the same mound which yielded the bird vessel of Squier and Davis' fame. The second vessel, a sand-tempered, simple-stamped, tetrapodal pot, was found in Mound City-13.

Beyond these data, the only point of interest in Mills' report is the statement that "The ceramic art seems to have occupied an important place in the economy of primitive man of the Mound City group" (Mills, 1922:509). With reference to Scioto ware, and possibly to some of the Southeastern Series sherds, Mills adds that this " . . . ware, in fragments, was found rather freely in several mounds of the group, and doubtless represented vessels used ordinarily as containers, cooking pots, and so forth. This utility ware has been found in practically all the mounds of the culture examined . . . " (Mills, 1922:509).

As a further comment, one might note that Mound City was the one and only locality at which complete vessels were found in relatively large numbers dispersed through several different mounds. At least four vessels, none of which belong in the Scioto Series were found here; all occurred in apparently ceremonial contexts.

Analysis: Mound City-2

Hopewellian Series, Biglobular (Bird) Vessel—1

Vessel, Limestone:	1 (--)

Hopewellian and Southeastern Series, Untyped Bird Vessel—1 (Pl. 11,*a*)
Vessel, Limestone: 1 (--)
(tetrapodal, zoned)

Comments

The two vessels on record from this mound were found by the Squier and Davis and Mills surveys respectively. The precise provenience within the mound of the Squier and Davis vessel is uncertain; the Mills pot was found in "crematory No. 2" which ". . . contained no cremated remains, but a quantity of broken potteryware taken from it proved to be, upon restoration, a single vessel . . . " (Mills, 1922:443).

Both of these curious vessels are decorated with bird designs. The Squier and Davis birds have hooked bills and appear to represent raptorial birds. The Mills birds show flattened broad bills with nostrils, suggesting the shoveler duck. Seip-1 produced a sherd of a similar vessel. The treatment of both, the Mound City and Seip specimens, shows other similarities. In both cases the background consists of plain dentate-stamping. The illustration of the Squier and Davis vessel does not make clear the nature of the background treatment, though it appears to have been similar. This vessel is now deposited in the British Museum. While the original illustration (Squier and Davis, 1848, Pl. XLVII, 2) does not show this, Dr. J. B. Griffin of the University of Michigan, who has seen the original, has been able to establish that this was originally a biglobular pot, the upper part of which is broken (personal communication). Both vessels are small, the Mills specimen being approximately 12 cms in height.

Of great interest is the fact that the Mills vessel combines attributes of both, the Southeastern Series (tetrapodal supports) and the Hopewellian Series (zoned design, stamping, birds). In addition, its body is square; this is a unique feature not noted on any other Ohio Hopewell vessel.

Both specimens may have been imports; they do not seem to fit the usual Ohio evidence. They bear close resemblance to Marksville types. The relevant elements are the bird designs and, as far as the Mills pot is concerned, also the rim treatment which consists of straight, vertical dentate-stamping.

Analysis: Mound City-3

Hopewellian Series, Chillicothe Rocker-stamped—1
D. Dentate Rocked: 1
Vessel, Grit: 1 (--)
(zoned)

PLATE 11

a

b

Mound City-2 (*a*) Bird Vessel. Mound City-13; (*b*) Turner Simple-stamped *B*. (Photographs by Ohio State Museum.)

Comments

This vessel was excavated by Squier and Davis (1848, Pl. XLVII, 1). The precise provenience unit is not known. The vessel is now in the British Museum. It is zoned and has a flat bottom. Again, as in the case of the Mound City-2 vessel, this specimen may be an imported item. Certainly, the rim treatment is entirely alien to classic Hopewellian pottery in Ohio.

Analysis: Mound City-13

Southeastern Series, Turner Simple-stamped *B*—1 (Pl. 11, *b*)
Vessel, Sand: 1 (Rim: 3 mm; body: 4-5 mm)
(tetrapodal)

Comments

Mound City 13 is the famed structure which contained the mica grave. The single identified pot from this tumulus was found in a ceremonial deposit on the floor of the mound. In conformity with sherds from apparently similar vessels found at various sites, the neck and rim sections are plain. They are separated from the stamped body by a band of hemiconical punctates. The dimensions are: height-11.8 cms; maximum width—12.2 cms; length of tetrapodal supports—0.7 cms.

Analysis: Mound City-general

Scioto Series, McGraw Cord-marked—152 (Fig. 10, A-E; Pl. 12, *a-e*)
Body sherds, Grit: 18 (2- 6 mm; 4.3 mm)
Limestone: 131 (2- 9 mm; 4.8 mm)
(lobed: 1)
Rim sherds, Grit: 3 (8-11 mm; 7.5 mm)

Scioto Series, McGraw Plain—123 (Fig. 10, F-K; 11, G-H)
Body sherds, Grit: 86 (2- 9 mm; 5.0 mm)
Limestone: 12 (3- 8 mm; 5.3 mm)
Rim sherds, Grit: 10 (4-12 mm; 5.7 mm)
Limestone: 15 (4- 6 mm; 6.0 mm)

Hopewellian Series, Chillicothe Rocker-stamped—6
A. Plain-rocked: 1
Body sherds, Grit: 1 (6 mm)
(zoned: 1)
D. Dentate-rocked: 5 (Pl. 13, *f*)
Body sherds, Limestone: 5 (3- 7 mm; 5.8 mm)
(zoned: 5)

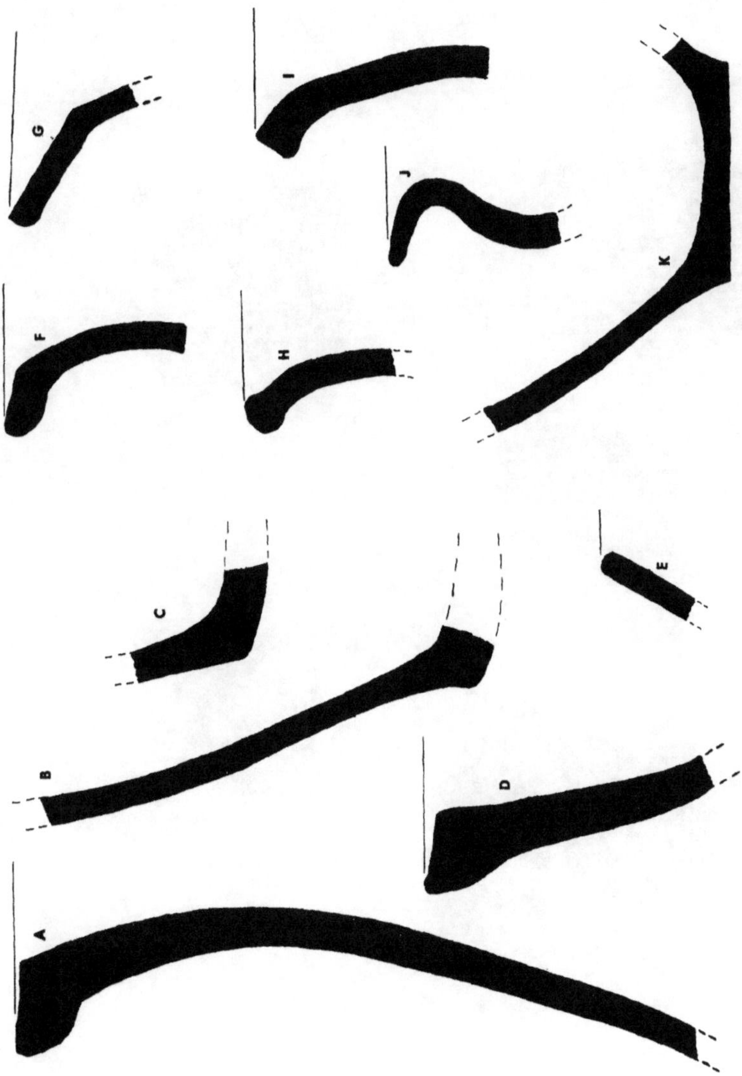

Fig. 10. Mound City General. (A-E) McGraw Cord-marked; (F-K) McGraw Plain.

PLATE 12

Mound City General. (*a–e*) McGraw Cord-marked.

Hopewellian Series, Chillicothe Brushed—1
Body sherds, Limestone: 1 (5 mm)
(zoned: 1)

Hopewellian Series, Untyped Dentate-stamped—8 (Fig. 11, D; Pl. 13, *b–e*)
Body sherds, Limestone: 7 (4- 5 mm; 4.6 mm)
(zoned: 7)
Rim sherds, Limestone: 1 (5 mm)

Hopewellian Series, Brangenberg Plain—1 (Fig. 11, C)
Rim sherds, Grit: 1 (13 mm)

Hopewellian Series, Seip Plain—2 (Fig. 11, A-B)
Rim sherds, Grit: 2 (6 mm)

Hopewellian Series, Untyped Zoned Incised—6 (Pl. 13, *g*)
Body sherds, Grit: 2 (3- 9 mm; 6.0 mm)
Limestone: 4 (4- 6 mm; 5.0 mm)

Hopewellian Series, Hopewell Rims—3 (Fig. 11, E-F; Pl. 13, *a*)
Grit: 3 (7.0 mm)

Southeastern Series, Turner Simple-stamped *B*—1 (Pl. 14, *a–c*, Fig. 1)
Body sherds, Sand: 7 (3- 5 mm; 4.5 mm)

Total 309 sherds
Grand Total 313 sherds

Comments

The Scioto Series conforms to the type definitions. The only point of note is the presence in many of the limestone-tempered sherds of some grit and mica particles. This is not called mixed temper, because the amounts of extraneous additives do not seem to warrant this. In the main, the Scioto Series sherds are quite thin.

In the Hopewellian Series the plain dentate-stamped sherds are somewhat unusual. They range in color from orange-buff to blue-grey. Temper particles are small, and the sherds are very hard and moderately polished. The decorations, consisting of undefined zoned designs, are carefully executed. The zones are filled with fine, plain dentate-stamping. The vessel from Mound City-2 found by Mills shows similar treatment; so does the bird vessel sherd from Seip-1. On the whole, and compared with the rest of the Hopewellian Series sherds from Ohio, this material does not appear to be local. Its closest relative appears to be in the Marksville Stamped series from the lower Mississippi Valley.

The Untyped Zoned sherds of the Hopewellian Series correspond in most respects to other standard Ohio Hopewell pottery,

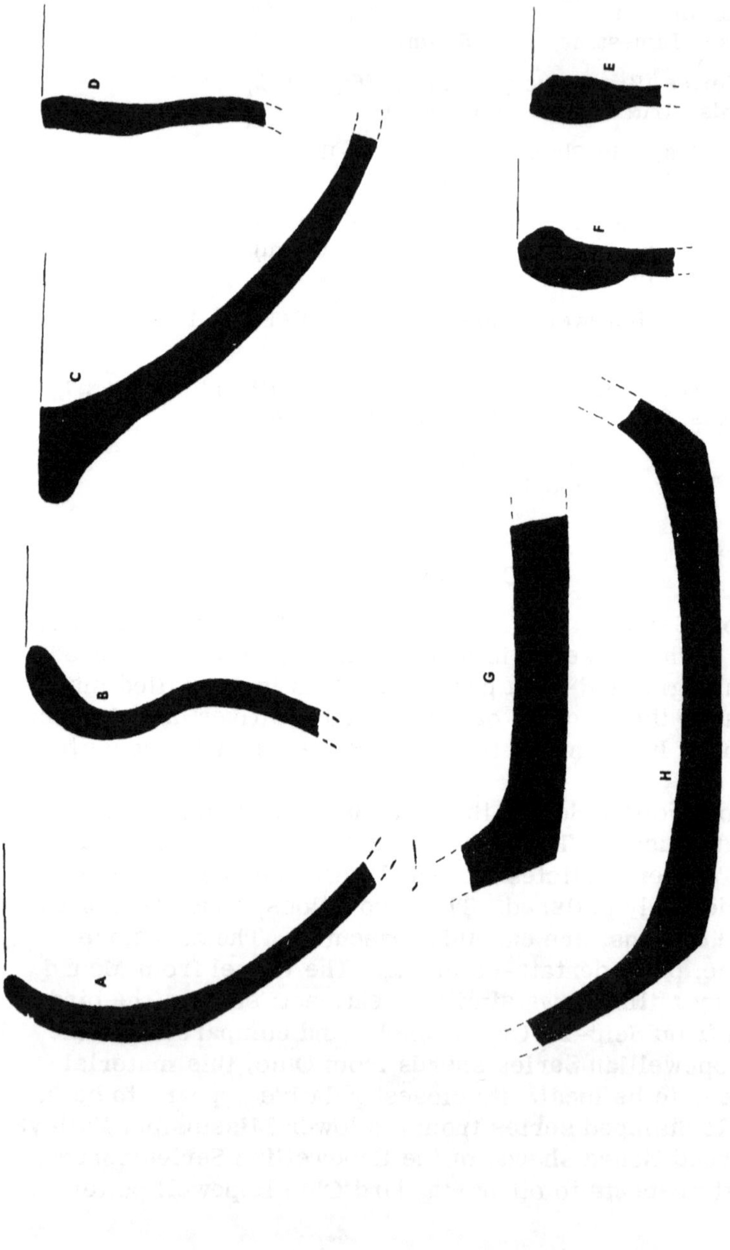

Fig. 11. Mound City General. (A–B) Seip Plain; (C) Brangenberg Plain; (D) Hopewellian Series, Untyped Dentate-stamped (on rim); (E–F) Hopewell Rims; (G–H) McGraw Plain.

PLATE 13

Mound City General. (*a*) Hopewell Rim; (*b–e*) Hopewellian Series, Untyped Dentate-stamped; (*f*) Chillicothe Rocker Stamped, dentate-rocked; (*g*) Hopewellian Series, Untyped Zoned Incised.

PLATE 14

Fig. 1. Mound City General. (*a–c*) Turner Simple-stamped *B*.

Fig. 2. Seip-1. (*a* = unit 237/8) Hopewell Rim; (*b* = unit 237/8); (*c* = unit 237/8) Chillicothe Rocker-stamped, plain-rocked; (*d* = unit 161) McGraw Cord-marked.

though qualitatively they are better than, for example the broken-down material from such sites as Turner and McGraw; but this applies to the remainder of the Mound City Hopewellian Series as well. The zoned incisions are deep and broad; they give the impression of having been executed with a steady and secure hand.

The distribution of the various ceramic series from Mound City General is as follows:

	Percent	Sherds
Scioto Series:	89.00	275
Hopewellian Series:	8.73	27
Southeastern Series:	2.26	7

Within the Scioto Series (N = 275) the distribution of McGraw Cord-marked and McGraw Plain is as follows:

	Percent	Sherds
McGraw Cord-marked:	55.27	152
McGraw Plain:	44.72	123

The distribution of temper for the total series is as follows:

	Percent	Sherds
Grit:	40.77	126
Limestone:	56.95	176
Sand:	2.26	7

There is a slight discrepancy between the findings presented here and those reported by Griffin for Mound City (1945:241). This pertains especially to the matter of temper. Griffin reports 38 per cent limestone and 60 per cent grit. Since the data given by Griffin otherwise agree with the present ones within a range of 2 per cent, I suggest that the major inversion as far as tempering material is concerned, may be the result of different classifications of the sherds with somewhat mixed temper alluded to earlier.

SEIP

The earliest major exploration of the Seip group of earthworks in Ross County, Ohio, was carried out by Squier and Davis (1848), although Caleb Atwater (1820) had already given a description of these structures. The first systematic excavations were undertaken for the Ohio Historical Society by Mills in what later became known as Seip-2, one of the two very large tumuli associated with the earthworks (Mills, 1909). Originally this structure was named Seip-1—at least this is the designation that occurs on a number of sherds that came demonstrably from this mound. Between 1925 and 1929 Shetrone and Greenman carried out excavations in the second, larger mound which they named Seip-1 (Shetrone and Greenman, 1931). This reversed numbering system has been a cause of constant irritation in the present analysis.

Before discussing the ceramic evidence given in the two site reports and in the Ohio State Museum catalogue, a brief commentary is required on the manner in which the Seip material is preserved and catalogued in the Ohio State Museum. Since the published references on pottery are scanty indeed, it was necessary to combine them with available catalogue data, that is, the catalogue and accession numbers, and with occasional inked notations on the sherds themselves.

All the Seip material is catalogued under No. 957, regardless of mound provenience. This means that a vast number of sherds which can not, (a) be equated with illustrated or other identified specimens, or which (b) do not bear catalogue subnumbers, must be regarded as having been obtained from Seip-General. Here included are sherds which demonstrably were found, but not so marked, under the embankment of the earthworks.

With one exception, the material from Mills' earlier excavations of Seip-2 bears no subnumbers at all. This is also true of the majority of sherds recovered during Shetrone and Greenman's subsequent expedition to Seip-1. However, a number of sherds from this enterprise do bear subnumbers which not only identify them as coming from Seip-1, but which also indicate specific excavation units and features. Unfortunately, it is quite clear from the evidence of matching sherds, that these provenience unit data may not be trustworthy throughout. Repeatedly matching sherds with differing subnumbers representing diverse features were encountered during the ceramic analysis. Whether this is evidence for a mix-up during cataloguing, or whether matching sherds legitimately occurred in quite different features, can no longer be established at this late date. With one exception, where sherds from two features fairly consistently could be matched, the Seip-1 material will here be discussed by the supposed provenience units.

Another point of importance is the fact that because of the relative abundance of pottery from Seip, the collection became an inexhaustable source for sample collections. While I know of a number of such collections in various institutions, it did not prove feasible to examine them. What should be kept in mind is that such collections generally were slanted toward classic Hopewell sherds, rather than toward the unspectacular items of the Scioto Series. Hence the statistics on relative proportions within the various ceramic series almost certainly do not reflect the true distribution of these wares.

Finally, there are some sherds which in one way or another could be identified as having been found at a location 800 feet northeast of the mounds (cat. no. 957/257) and in a field "near fishing camp" within the enclosure (cat. no. 957/246). According to a personal communication from the late R. Goslin of the Ohio State Museum, these locations are identical with excavations carried out under the enclosure of the earthwork.

Analysis: Seip-1

Shetrone and Greenman's report on the excavations at Seip-1 contains numerous references to, as well as a special section on, the pottery from this mound (1931:430–38). The statistics given here are not particularly relevant, since it is not possible to sort out the finds from the various site excavations. Similarly, the typological breakdown, in the light of modern knowledge, is woefully inadequate. Still, for completeness' sake, the data will here be given summarily; Shetrone and Greenman distinguish the following classes of pottery:

"Ceremonial pottery" (Hopewellian and S. E. Series): 593 sherds
"Utility ware" (Scioto series): 235 sherds

It is stated that sherds were found on the floor of the mound in the three major refuse pits, with the "Burnt Offering," and on the platforms of several burials. The above statistics cannot be accurate since they are belied by the quantitative evidence from the collection itself.

In addition, eighty sherds (seven of which are classed as "ceremonial pottery") were found " . . . in a portion of the great wall of the Seip Group . . . at a depth of two feet in an ash deposit" (Shetrone and Greenman, 1931:438). In the following discussion all but four of these sherds seem to be submerged in the bulk of the Seip ceramics with the ubiquitous catalogue number 957; hence, they have to be listed under the discussion of the Seip-General material.

To some extent it has been possible to equate the sherds from Seip-1 on the basis of subcatalogue numbers from specific provenience units. The following are the relevant data:

Unit 957/161: This refers to three depressions in the floor of the mound. They appear to have had some ceremonial significance, because their content appeared to have been purposely "killed" (Shetrone and Greenman, 1931:367, 432-33).

Units 957/237 and 957/238: These are "Two pits, four feet apart, extended beneath the floor just north of burials 95 and 96, one of them lying directly beneath burial 93" (Shetrone and Greenman, 1931:368). Many of the sherds from the two pits could be matched, regardless of their supposed provenience.

Unit 957/216: This is a pit near burial 77. "In Burial 77 the cremated remains of an adult lay 14 inches beneath the floor of the mound on a roughly circular clay "post" or knob about a foot in diameter, which rose from the bottom of a pit two feet four inches in depth and four feet seven inches in diameter. In this pit were a large number of deer bones, about a dozen pot-sherds of both ceremonial and utility type, and a sheet of uncut mica, all intermingled with ashes, charcoal and black humus" (Shetrone and Greenman, 1931:475).

Unit 957/248: Burial 85. This was a submound burial.

Unit 957/260: The location is burial 72 which was associated with the rich burial 73, both being located under a primary mound.

Unit: Burial 83. Provenience inked on sherds.

Unit: Burial 53. Provenience inked on sherds.

Unit: Burial 48. Provenience inked on sherds.

Unit: Burial 88. Provenience inked on sherds.

Unit: Burial 56. Provenience inked on sherds.

Unit: Burnt Offering. Provenience cross-referenced in site report.

Unit 957/161

Scioto Series, McGraw Cord-marked—129 (Fig. 12, A, C; Pl. 14, *d*, Fig. 2)
    Body sherds, Grit: 128 (4- 7 mm; 4.7 mm)
    Rim sherds, Grit: 1 (8 mm)

Scioto Series, McGraw Plain—14
    Body sherds, Grit: 5 (3- 8 mm; 5.6 mm)
        Limestone: 6 (4- 8 mm; 5.8 mm)
    Rim sherds, Grit: 3 (7- 8 mm; 7.6 mm)

Hopewellian Series, Chillicothe Rocker-stamped—20
    D. Dentate-rocked: 20
        Body sherds; Grit: 19 (3- 5 mm; 3.7 mm)
            (zoned: 2)
        Rim sherds, Grit: 1 (4 mm)

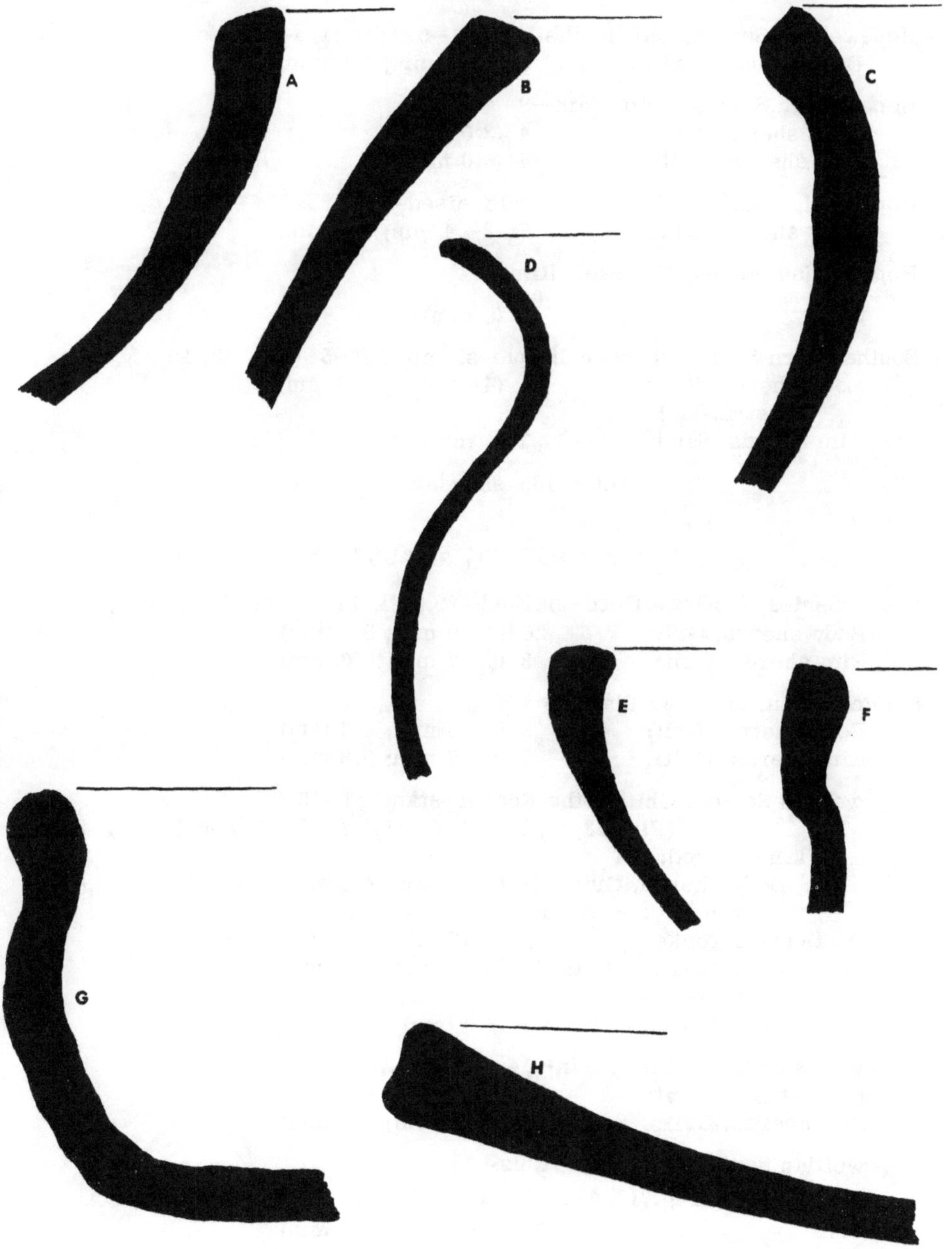

Fig. 12. Seip-1. (A,C = unit 161; B = unit 216) McGraw Cord-marked; (D = unit 161) Turner Simple-stamped *B*; (E = unit 237/8; F = unit 216) Seip Plain; (G = unit 216) McGraw Plain; (H = unit 237/8) Untyped Platter.

Hopewellian Series, Chillicothe Incised—6 (Pl. 21, *d–e*)
Body sherds, Grit: 6 (4- 7 mm; 5.0 mm)

Hopewellian Series, Seip Plain—8
Body sherds, Grit: 4 (3.0 mm)
Rim sherds, Grit: 4 (6.0 mm)

Hopewellian Series, Untyped Zoned Incised—6
Body sherds, Grit: 6 (3- 4 mm; 3.5 mm)

Hopewellian Series, Hopewell Rims—1
Grit: 1 (5 mm)

Southeastern Series, Turner Simple-stamped *B*—5 (Fig. 12, D)
Body sherds, Sand: 4 (4- 5 mm; 4.5 mm)
(tetrapodal: 1)
Rim sherds, Sand: 1 (4 mm)

Total 189 sherds

Units 957/237 and 957/238

Scioto Series, McGraw Cord-marked—29 (Pl. 14, *b*; Fig. 2; Pl. 19 *a*)
Body sherds, Grit: 26 (3- 9 mm; 5.4 mm)
Rim sherds, Grit: 3 (5- 7 mm; 6.0 mm)

Scioto Series, McGraw Plain—6
Body sherds, Grit: 3 (3- 6 mm; 4.3 mm)
Rim sherds, Grit: 3 (6- 7 mm; 5.3 mm)

Hopewellian Series, Chillicothe Rocker-stamped—75
(Fig. 13, G; Pl. 14, *c*; Fig. 2; Pl. 17 *a–d*; Pl. 18)
A. Plain-rocked: 31
Body sherds, Grit: 31 (3- 6 mm; 4.2 mm)
(zoned: 28; lobed: 2)
D. Dentate-rocked: 43 (Pl. 16; Pl. 19 *b–c*; Pl. 20, *c*)
Body sherds, Grit: 41 (3- 6 mm; 4.2 mm)
(zoned: 12)
Rim sherds, Grit: 3 (6.0 mm)

Hopewellian Series, Seip Plain—14 (Fig. 12, E)
Body sherds, Grit: 11 (3- 6 mm; 4.6 mm)
Rim sherds, Grit: 3 (6- 7 mm; 6.7 mm)

Hopewellian Series, Hopewell Rims—15
(Fig. 13, A–F; Pl. 14, *a*; Fig. 2; Pl. 15, *a–b*)
Grit: 15 (5- 8 mm; 5.9 mm)

Southeastern Series, Turner Simple-stamped *B*—1
Body sherds, Sand: 1 (4 mm)

Unknown Series, Cord-marked and Plain Platters—28 (Fig. 12, H)
Body sherds, Grit: 12 (5- 8 mm; 5.8 mm)
(cord-marked: 3; plain: 9)

Rim sherds, Grit: 16 (5-12 mm; 10.0 mm)
(cord-marked: 6; plain: 10)

Total 168 sherds

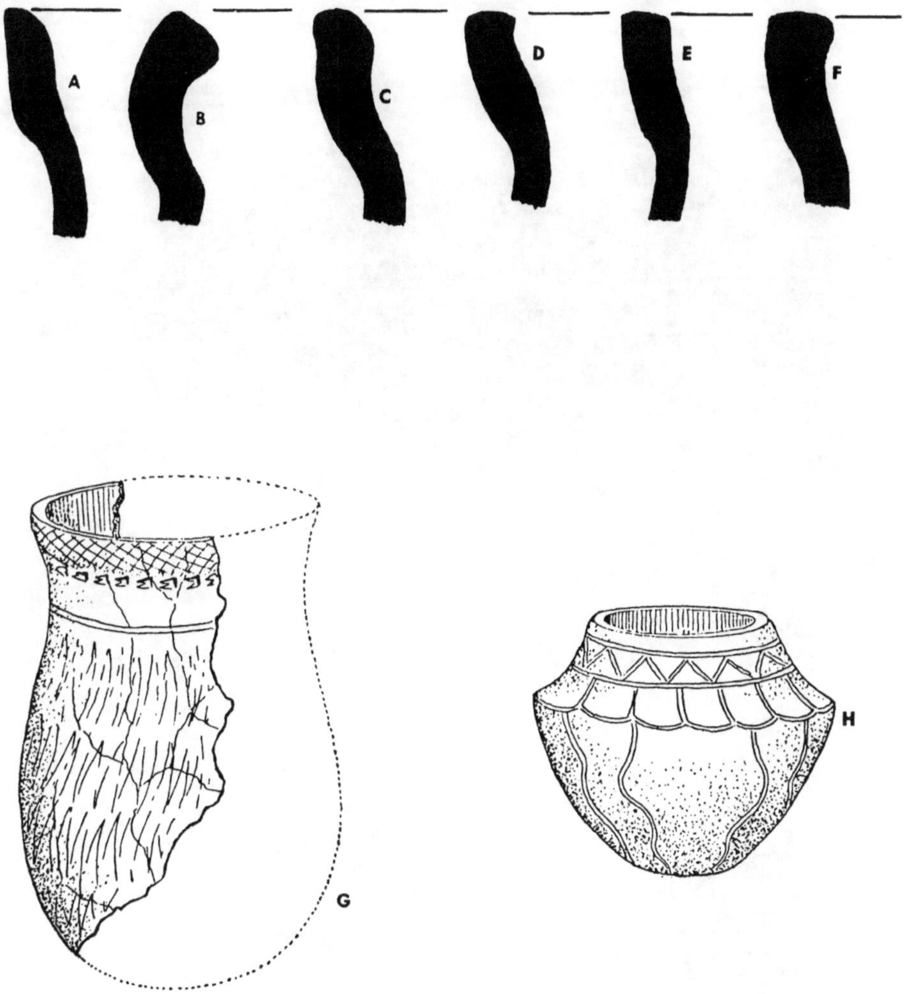

Fig. 13. Seip-1. (A-F = unit 237/8) Hopewell Rims; (G = unit 237/8) Chillicothe Rocker-stamped, Plain-rocked; (H = unit Burnt Offering) Incised Miniature Vessel; (G-H: after Shetsone and Greenman, 1931).

PLATE 15

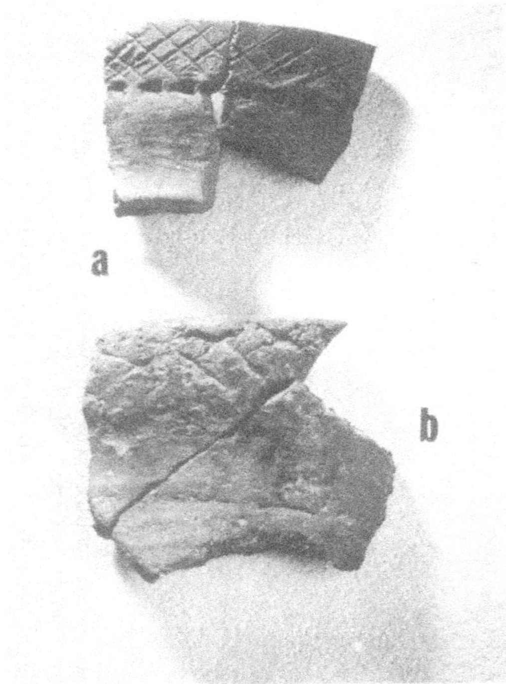

Seip-1. (*a–b* = unit 237/8) Hopewell Rims.

PLATE 16

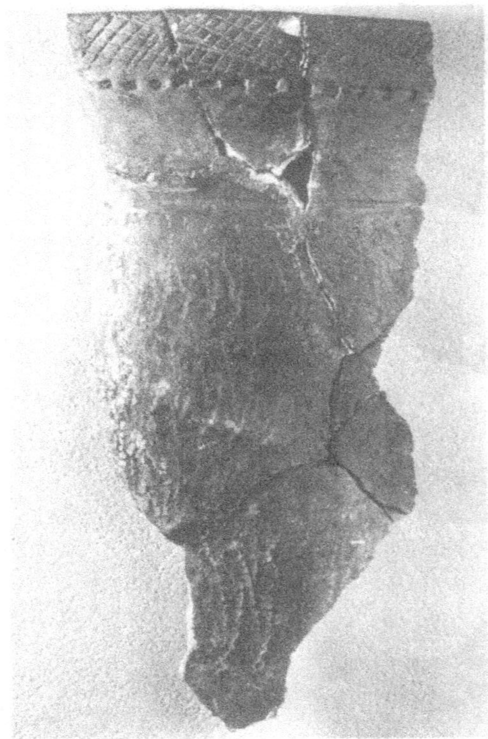

Seip-1. (unit 231/8) Chillicothe Rocker-stamped, dentate-rocked.

PLATE 17

Seip-1. (*a–d* = unit 237/8) Chillicothe Rocker-stamped, plain-rocked.

PLATE 18

Seip-1. (unit 237/8) Chillicothe Rocker-stamped, plain-rocked.

PLATE 19

Seip-1. (*a* = unit 237/8) McGraw Cord-marked; (*b–c* = unit 237/8) Chillicothe Rocker-stamped, dentate-rocked.

PLATE 20

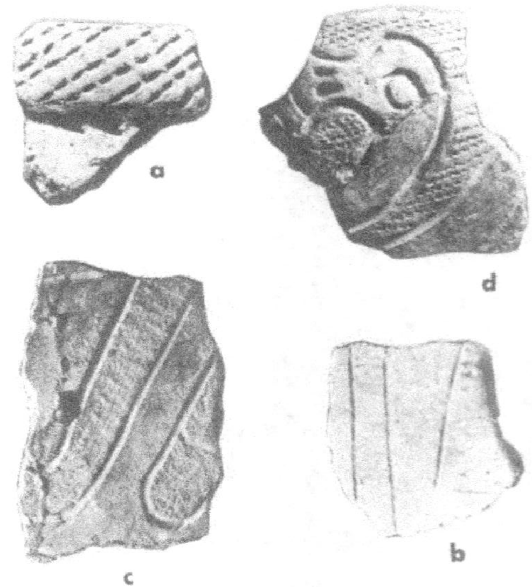

Seip General. (*a*) Hopewellian Series, Untyped Dentate-stamped; (*b*) Chillicothe Rocker-stamped, plain rocked. Seip-2. (*c*) Bird Vessel. Seip-1. (*d* = unit 237/8) Chillicothe Rocker-stamped, dentate-rocked.

PLATE 21

Seip-2. (*a*) Turner Simple-stamped *B*. Seip General. (*b–c*) Southeastern Series, Untyped Incised. Seip-1. (*d–e* = unit 161) Chillicothe Incised.

Unit 957/216

Scioto Series, McGraw Cord-marked—22 (Fig. 12, B)
Body sherds, Grit: 21 (2-11 mm; 5.2 mm)
Rim sherds, Grit: 1 (6 mm)

Scioto Series, McGraw Plain—8 (Fig. 12, G)
Body sherds, Grit: 5 (3- 7 mm; 5.5 mm)
Rim sherds, Grit: 2 (5- 9 mm; 7.0 mm)
Miniature pot, Grit: 1 (rim: 9 mm; body: 12 mm)

Hopewellian Series, Chillicothe Rocker-stamped—2
D. Dentate-rocked: 2
Body sherds, Grit: 2 (5.0 mm)

Hopewellian Series, Seip Plain—15 (Fig. 12, F)
Body sherds, Grit: 11 (4- 5 mm; 4.6 mm)
Rim sherds, Grit: 4 (7- 8 mm; 7.1 mm)

Southeastern Series, Turner Simple-stamped *A*—1
Body sherds, Grit: 1 (6 mm)

Unknown Series, Cord-marked and Plain Platters—3
Rim sherds, Grit: 3 (5- 6 mm; 5.3 mm)
(cord-marked: 3)

Unknown Series, Miniature Incised Vessel—1
Vessel, Grit: 1 (4 mm)

Total 52 sherds

Unit 957/260

Scioto Series, McGraw Cord-marked—2
Body sherds, Grit: 2 (5.0 mm)

Southeastern Series, Turner Simple-stamped *B*—1
Body sherds, Sand: 1 (6 mm)

Total 3 sherds

Unit 957/248

Scioto Series, McGraw Cord-marked—2
Body sherds, Grit: 1 (5 mm)
Rim sherds, Grit: 1 (5 mm)

Unit: Burial 53

Hopewellian Series, Untyped Zoned Incised—1
Body sherds, Grit: 1 (7 mm)

Unit: Burial 48

Scioto Series, McGraw Cord-marked—1
Body sherds, Grit: 1 (unmeasurable)

Unit: Burial 88

Scioto Series, McGraw Cord-marked—2
Body sherds, Grit: 2 (4.0 mm)

Hopewellian Series, Chillicothe Rocker-stamped—3
A. Plain-rocked: 3
Body sherds, Grit: 3 (4- 6 mm; 5.0 mm)
(zoned: 1)

Hopewellian Series, Hopewell Rims—1
Grit: 1 (5 mm)

Total 6 sherds

Unit: Burial 83

Hopewellian Series, Chillicothe Rocker-stamped—1
D. Dentate-rocked: 1
Body sherds, Grit: 1 (3 mm)

Unit: Burial 56

Hopewellian Series, Seip Plain—1
Body sherds, Grit: 1 (3 mm)

Unit: Burnt Offering

Unknown Series, Incised Miniature Vessel—1 (Fig. 13, H)
Body sherds, Grit: 1 (--)

Grand Total 425 sherds

Comments

Details of the ceramic material from Seip-1 will be dis- under Seip-General, because the bulk of those sherds obviously came from this mound as well. The distribution of the various ceramic series at Seip-1 is as follows:

	Percent	Sherds
Scioto Series:	50.59	215
Hopewellian Series:	39.76	169
Southeastern Series:	1.88	8
Other:	7.76	33

Within the Scioto Series (N = 215) the distribution of McGraw Cord-marked and McGraw Plain is as follows:

	Percent	Sherds
McGraw Cord-marked:	86.97	187
McGraw Plain:	13.02	28

The temper distribution for the total series is as follows:

	Percent	Sherds
Grit:	97.17	413
Limestone:	1.41	6
Sand:	1.41	6

Analysis: Seip-2

Pottery appears to have been scarce at this mound. This can be inferred from Mills' cogitations. He says: "It seems strange that a people well versed in the fictile art . . . would not in some way employ this art facility in their mortuary customs" (1909: 317). The only other reference, apart from a few illustrations (Fig. 39), is the statement that "Fragments of broken pottery were found in almost every portion of the mound, and in several instances, potsherds of good size, and representing a high type of fictile art, were found in several of the graves, but were not associated with the charred remains" (Mills, 1909:317).

Several of the sherds illustrated by Mills were found in the extant collection. In addition, some sherds from this mound bear the inked notation "Mound-1" (and this includes Mills' illustrated specimens) indicative of their provenience. Since this notation usually is accompanied by an additional notation of the year in which the sherds were excavated, it is obvious that, in terms of Shetrone and Greenman's revised mound nomenclature for Seip, it refers to Seip-2. In the Ohio State Museum catalogue only one subnumbered reference correlates ceramics with a feature; this reads 957/282 and refers to burial 85.

Unit 957/282

Scioto Series, McGraw Cord-marked—2
Body sherds, Grit: 2 (5.0 mm)

Scioto Series, McGraw Plain—1
Rim sherds, Grit: 1 (8 mm)

Southeastern Series, Untyped Complicated-stamped—2
Body sherds, Sand: 1 (8 mm)
Limestone: 1 (8 mm)

Southeastern Series, Untyped Cord-marked—1
Body sherds, Grit: 1 (--)
(tetrapod)

Southeastern Series, Untyped Plain—1
Body sherd, Sand: 1 (8 mm)

Total 7 sherds

Unit: General

Scioto Series, McGraw Cord-marked—7
Body sherds, Grit: 7 (3- 7 mm; 5.3 mm)

Scioto Series, McGraw Plain—3
Body sherds, Grit: 2 (9.0 mm)
Limestone: 1 (8 mm)

Hopewellian Series, Chillicothe Rocker-stamped—6
A. Plain-rocked: 3
Body sherds, Grit: 3 (4- 6 mm; 5.0 mm)
(zoned: 3)
D. Dentate-rocked: 3
Body sherds, Grit: 2 (4- 5 mm; 4.5 mm)
(zoned: 2)
Rim sherds, Grit: 1 (5 mm)

Hopewellian Series, Bird vessel—1 (Pl. 20, *c*)
Body sherds, Grit: 1 (4 mm)

Hopewellian Series, Hopewell Rims—2
Grit: 2 (5.0 mm)

Southeastern Series, Turner Simple-stamped *A*—1
Body sherds, Grit: 1 (7 mm)

Southeastern Series, Turner Simple-stamped *B*—6 (Pl. 21, *a*)
Body sherds, Sand: 6 (5- 7 mm; 5.6 mm)
(tetrapods: 1)

Southeastern Series, Untyped Complicated-stamped—5 (Pl. 22, *c,e,f*)
Body sherds, Sand: 5 (5- 8 mm; 6.6 mm)

Southeastern Series, Untyped Diamond Check-stamped—8 (Pl. 23)
Body sherds, Sand: 8 (6- 9 mm; 7.6 mm)

Total 39 sherds
Grand Total 46 sherds

Comments

The fabrics and decorations of the Hopewellian Series are excellent, nearly approaching Illinoian standards. The sherds are all moderately polished. One of the Hopewell Rims bears traces of a very finely incised pattern imitating rocker-stamping on the interior surface. The Bird vessel sherd represents a conventionalized spoonbill. The background is covered with plain dentate-stamping. Temper is very fine, and the color is light yellow-buff;

PLATE 22

Seip-2. (*a–b*) Southeastern Series, Untyped Simple-stamped. (*c,e,f*) Southeastern Series, Untyped Complicated-stamped. Seip General.

PLATE 23

Seip-2. (*a*) Southeastern Series, Untyped Diamond-Check-stamped.

PLATE 24

Seip General. (*a,c,e-f*) Chillicothe Rocker-stamped, plain-rocked; (*b,d*) dentate-rocked.

the fabric is extremely hard and well fired. This would seem to be a trade item, possibly of Marksville origin.

The Diamond Check-stamped sherds are similar to those few finds noted from a number of other Ohio Hopewell sites such as Rockhold and Harness. As usual, the sherds are thick, hard, and the decorations have been almost entirely eliminated by smoothing. The Complicated-stamped sherds are hard, generally dark, almost black in color. Almost certainly they are not local products. The single Southeastern Series Plain sherd has a row of rectangular punctates at the body-neck junction.

The distribution of the various ceramic series from Seip-2 is as follows:

	Percent	Sherds
Scioto Series:	28.26	13
Hopewellian Series:	19.56	9
Southeastern Series:	52.17	24

Within the Scioto Series (N = 13) the distribution of McGraw Cord-marked and McGraw Plain is as follows:

	Percent	Sherds
McGraw Cord-marked:	69.22	9
McGraw Plain:	30.77	4

The temper distribution for the total series is as follows:

	Percent	Sherds
Grit:	50.00	23
Limestone:	4.34	2
Sand:	45.65	21

Analysis: Seip-Enclosure

Scioto Series, McGraw Cord-marked—4

Body sherds, Grit:	1 (7 mm)
Limestone:	1 (8 mm)
Rim sherds, Grit:	2 (7- 9 mm; 8.0 mm)

Comments

The Scioto Series constitutes 100 per cent of the sample; within the series McGraw Cord-marked also constitutes 100 per cent. Grit temper accounts for 75 per cent and limestone temper for 25 per cent.

Analysis: Seip-General

Scioto Series, McGraw Cord-marked—2020 (Fig. 14, A-H)
    Body sherds, Grit: 2001 (2-10 mm; 5.9 mm)
    Rim sherds, Grit: 17 (6-11 mm; 8.3 mm)
        Limestone: 2 (5 mm)

Scioto Series, McGraw Plain—202 (Fig. 15, A-I)
    Body sherds, Grit: 139 (3-14 mm; 5.9 mm)
        Limestone: 14 (4-10 mm; 6.7 mm)
    Rim sherds, Grit: 46 (3-11 mm; 5.3 mm)
        Limestone: 3 (5- 6 mm; 5.3 mm)

Hopewellian Series, Chillicothe Rocker-stamped—163
    A. Plain-rocked: 37 (Pl. 20, *b*; Pl. 25, *b-c*; Pl. 24, *a, c, e-f*)
        Body sherds, Grit: 37 (3- 6 mm; 4.5 mm)
    D. Dentate-rocked: 126 (Pl. 20, *d*; Pl. 25, *a, d*; Pl. 24, *b, d*)
        Body sherds, Grit: 125 (3- 6 mm; 4.0 mm)
        Rim sherds, Grit: 1 (8 mm)
            (zoned: 1)

Hopewellian Series, Seip Plain—49 (Fig. 15, L)
    Body sherds, Grit: 47 (3- 5 mm; 4.2 mm)
    Rim sherds, Grit: 2 (6- 8 mm; 7.0 mm)

Hopewellian Series, Untyped Dentate-stamped—1 (Pl. 20, *a*)
    Rim sherds, Grit: 1 (5 mm)

Hopewellian Series, Hopewell Rims—16 (Fig. 15, K)
    Grit: 16 (4- 8 mm; 5.8 mm)

Hopewellian Series, Unidentifiable Residue—5
    Body sherds, Grit: 5 (3- 6 mm; 5.2 mm)
        (zoned: 5)

Southeastern Series, Turner Simple-stamped *A*—22 (Fig. 16, B)
    Body sherds, Grit: 20 (3- 9 mm; 5.0 mm)
    Rim sherds, Grit: 2 (5- 7 mm; 6.0 mm)

Southeastern Series, Turner Simple-stamped *B*—12 (Fig. 16, C-D)
    Body sherds, Sand: 11 (3- 6 mm; 4.5 mm)
        (tetrapods: 1)
    Rim sherds, Sand: 1 (4 mm)

Southeastern Series, Untyped Simple-stamped—1 (Fig. 16, A; Pl. 22, *a,b*)
    Vessel, Grit: 1 (Rim: 13 mm; body: 9 mm)

Southeastern Series, Turner Check-stamped—1
    Body sherds, Limestone: 1 (6 mm)

Southeastern Series, Untyped Plain—2
    Body sherds, Grit: 2 (--)
        (tetrapods: 2)

Fig. 14. Seip General. (A–H) McGraw Cord-marked.

Fig. 15. Seip General. (A–I) McGraw Plain; (J) Unknown Series, Notched Rim; (K) Hopewell Rim; (L) Seip Plain; (M–N) Platters.

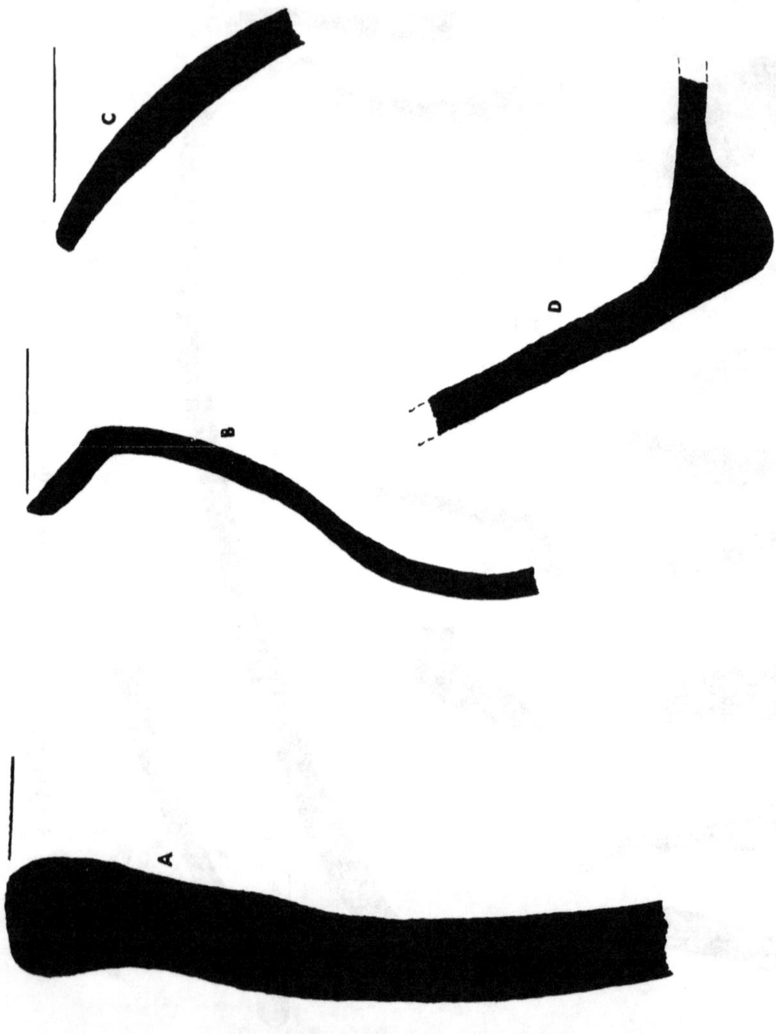

Fig. 16. Seip General. (A) Southeastern Series, Untyped Simple-stamped; (B) Turner Simple-stamped *A*; (C–D) Turner Simple-stamped *B*.

PLATE 25

Seip General. (*a,d*) Chillicothe Rocker-stamped dentate-rocked; (*b–c*) plain-rocked.

PLATE 26

Fort Ancient. (*a*) Chillicothe Rocker-stamped, plain-rocked; (*b*) Hopewell Rim.

Southeastern Series, Untyped Incised—5 (Pl. 21, *b–c*)
Body sherds, Sand: 3 (5- 6 mm; 5.3 mm)
Rim sherds, Sand: 2 (4- 5 mm; 4.5 mm)

Southeastern Series, Untyped Complicated-stamped—3
Body sherds, Limestone: 1 (6 mm)
Sand: 2 (6 mm)

Unknown Series, Cord-marked and Plain Platters—27 (Fig. 15, M-N)
Rim and body sherds, Grit: 27 (rim: 3-10 mm; 6.3 mm; body: 3- 8 mm; 5.7 mm)
(cord-marked: 13; plain: 14)

Miami Series, Unknown Punctate—1
Body sherds, Grit: 1 (4 mm)

Unknown Series, Untyped Notched Rim—1 (Fig. 15, J)
Grit: 1 (3 mm)

Total 2531 sherds

Comments

Since the material definitely attributable to Seip-1, and that which has been classed under Seip-General, seem essentially identical, the two units can be discussed here *in toto*. It is likely that the only major unit from Seip-2 that might be submerged in the unit Seip-General consists of Plain and Cord-marked Scioto Series sherds. On the other hand, the majority of the ceramics from the embankment would also seem to be submerged here. In view of the fact, however, that no distinctive differences of any kind show up within the established types and series here lumped under Seip-General, the possibility that such sherds from other provenience units are included in this lot does not seem to have classificatory significance. Similarly, since the ceramics from Seip-1 and Seip-General show no differences either, it seems safe to lump them here in the final discussion, especially since the bulk of the Seip-General sherds probably came from Seip-1, even though this cannot be proved beyond doubt.

The Scioto Series requires only a brief comment. The material is generally thin, much smoothed, and fairly crumbly. The only curiosity is a miniature vessel, five cms high and eight cms wide; this very crudely made bowl has no counterparts from other Ohio sites.

The Hopewellian Series is remarkable on several counts. Undoubtedly it represents the best expression of Hopewell ceramics in all of Ohio. Almost throughout, the sherds were made with great care. The fabrics are generally hard and well-fired. Most surfaces have moderate to high polish which in some cases, especially on the Seip Plain sherds amounts to almost a sheen. The decorations are carefully executed. Proportionately, zoning is more common at Seip than at any other Ohio site; the zones are complex, consisting of curvilinear and, less commonly, of angular patterns. Rim treatment is of high quality. Moderate interior grooving is common. The impression of rim thickening is often created by the exterior bulge produced by the interior groove. Smoothing after application of the decoration occurs in a high proportion of all sherds, especially in the case of the unzoned, dentate-rocked sherds. Here the rockered designs are often almost unrecognizable. Tempering particles range from very fine to medium; they are never densely distributed through the clay. The overall impression is one of fine tempering. Colors are predominantly in the light buff to red range on the zoned vessels, grading down to reddish and almost greenish-brown on the dentate-rocked sherds. With few exceptions vessel size is large, suggesting quasi-cylindrical, round-based, vessels.

A comment on the rocker-stamping is in order. First, the total absence of the fine, long Pike-related stamping must be noted. Still, within the stamping from Seip variations can be distinguished.

A. Plain Rocker-stamping:
  1. Made with a narrow- or broad-edged tool. The stamp is applied without dragging over the wet clay surface in the process of moving from one rocker-swing to the next.
  2. A tool similar to (1) is used, but the stamping edge, during the swing from rocker to rocker is dragged over the clay, thus producing an ill-defined impression which is very wide, and which shows the dragging marks of the stamping edge in the form of very narrowly spaced pseudo-dentate lines. These are nothing more than impressions of the slightly uneven surfaces of the stamping tools.

B. Dentate Rocker-stamping:
  1. A fine-toothed, but regularly spaced dentate tool, usually rather short, is used. The stamping process involves no dragging.
  2. A very fine-toothed stamping tool is used. This is invariably a short implement. The impressions are always applied by dragging the stamp lightly from swing to swing. (This type of impression can, on occasion, be mistaken for A-2 stamping.) In general, however, the matter can be decided on the grounds of the greater regularity of the dentate impressions in the case of true dentate rockering.

3. A coarse implement, with widely-spaced, often block-like dentations is used. The impressions are always very long, and they are never dragged. Thus, they are always clear, except when subsequent smoothing has altered them. Apparently, during the stamping process the ends of the stamping tools were firmly pressed into the wet clay during each rockering motion. These terminal impressions are, therefore, quite deep. Smoothing rarely eliminates them. As a result much smoothed sherds often convey at first sight the impression of being decorated with parallel rows of crude punctations.

These variations in rocker stamping at Seip are quite unique. At no other site have they been noted all together.

The Seip Plain sherds are of unusually high quality. Some of the clays used for most specimens are different from anything previously known from Ohio Hopewell sites. They are light colored, and almost sugary in consistency.

The Complicated-stamped sherds are similar to those from Seip-2. The curious Untyped Simple-stamped vessel requires comment. It consists of numerous sherds that must have been found in the same location. The fabric is coarse and brittle; the tempering particles of crushed rock are medium in size, and the color is an even grey. The walls are very thick, and the rim is straight-vertical with a flattened horizontal lip. The vessel must have been approximately 24 inches in height. The exterior surfaces, right up to the lip, are covered with carefully executed, deep, unsmoothed, horizontal simple-stamping of great regularity. I am not aware of any parallels to this vessel.

Another noteworthy feature of the Southeastern Series is the presence of a few sand tempered sherds with crudely incised decorations. These incisions are in the nature of cross-hatching which, when it occurs on rims, suggests Hopewellian affiliations; this may, however, be accidental, since the body sherds are similarly treated. As far as fabric, temper, etc. are concerned, these sherds are identical to those of Turner Simple-stamped *B*.

Finally, the residual materials deserve comment. Here, the platters are unique. They are large, shallow plates or dishes with straight, nearly horizontal, rims, and rounded bases. They occur with exterior cord-marking which is often smoothed, and plain. Plain sherds often show wiping marks on both exterior and interior faces. These marks are very prominent and must have been produced with a brush-like, coarse instrument. Generally, the platters are quite crumbly, consisting of poorly mixed and badly fired clays. Temper particles are medium sized.

Among the remaining sherds the two incised miniature vessels should be noted. Both specimens have precise provenience attributions. The complete vessel is seven cms high and nearly eight cms wide at the shoulder. The second, a fragmentary specimen, seems to have had about the same dimensions. The shoulders are sharply angular, the base nearly flat, and the neck slopes inward, terminating in a straight rim with a flat lip. The color is buff. The incisions are well executed, representing a design, identical on both vessels, which is totally alien to Hopewell (Fig. 13, H). The fabric is hard and well-fired, and the tempering particles are very fine.

Of the remaining two sherds the notched, everted, razor-edged rim has no parallels in Ohio Hopewell. The punctate sherd of the provisional Miami Series is similar to those from Turner, and conveys a late, Weaver-like impression. Unfortunately its provenience is not known.

The distribution of the various ceramic series from Seip-General is as follows:

	Percent	Sherds
Scioto Series:	87.79	2222
Hopewellian Series:	9.24	234
Southeastern Series:	1.82	46
Miami Series:	.04	1
Other:	1.10	29

Within the Scioto Series (N = 2222) the distribution of McGraw Cord-marked and McGraw Plain is as follows:

	Percent	Sherds
McGraw Cord-marked:	90.90	2020
McGraw Plain:	9.09	234

The temper distribution for the total series is as follows:

	Percent	Sherds
Grit:	98.42	2491
Limestone:	.83	21
Sand:	.75	19

The total sherd count for Seip is 3009. Griffin's brief published analysis of the Seip pottery (1945:241-42) does not indicate the size of the sample that was available at the time. In view of the fact that Seip material appears to have been frequently used for ceramic type collections and thus became dispersed, the differences between the present analysis and that carried out by Griffin may be explainable: the sample of 1945 may not have been identical in all respects with the sample examined nearly two decades later. The following are the discrepancies in the two analyses: Griffin notes 2 per cent limestone temper for the total series; the present survey only 1 per cent. According to Griffin cord-marked pottery amounted to 66 per cent and plain ware to 20 per cent of the total sample; in the present analysis these proportions were as follows: cord-marked pottery 73.77 per cent, plain ware 8.84 per cent.

FORT ANCIENT

This hilltop enclosure in Warren County, Ohio, was investigated on several occasions. The earlier excavations by Moorehead (1890, 1908) revealed Hopewellian burial mounds within the enclosure and outside. More recently, in 1939-40, Morgan found remains of a Hopewellian settlement outside the enclosure walls (Morgan, 1960). The following analysis is based on this work. The only reference in the literature to ceramics, other than sporadic mention of sherds, is contained in Morgan's brief description of the "fort" (1960:12). The sherds here discussed are deposited in the Ohio State Museum under catalogue number 1039.

Analysis

Scioto Series, McGraw Cord-marked—210
Body sherds, Grit: 210 (3- 8 mm; 5.4 mm)

Scioto Series, McGraw Plain—42 (Fig. 17, C)
Body sherds, Grit: 33 (4-10 mm; 5.4 mm)
Rim sherds, Grit: 9 (4- 8 mm; 5.6 mm)

Hopewellian Series, Chillicothe Rocker-stamped—19
A. Plain-rocked: 15 (Pl. 26, *a*)
Body sherds, Grit: 15 (3- 5 mm; 4.2 mm)
(zoned: 3)
D. Dentate-rocked: 4
Body sherds, Grit: 4 (4- 6 mm; 5.3 mm)

Hopewellian Series, Chillicothe Brushed—2
Body sherds, Grit: 2 (unmeasurable)
(zoned: 1)

Hopewellian Series, Brangenberg Plain—2 (Fig. 17, A)
Rim sherds, Grit: 2 (12-17 mm; 14.5 mm)
(red painted: 1)

Hopewellian Series, Untyped Zoned Incised—3
Body sherds, Grit: 3 (5- 6 mm; 5.6 mm)

Hopewellian Series, Hopewell Rims—3 (Fig. 17, B; Pl. 26, *b*)
Grit: 3 (7- 8 mm; 7.5 mm)

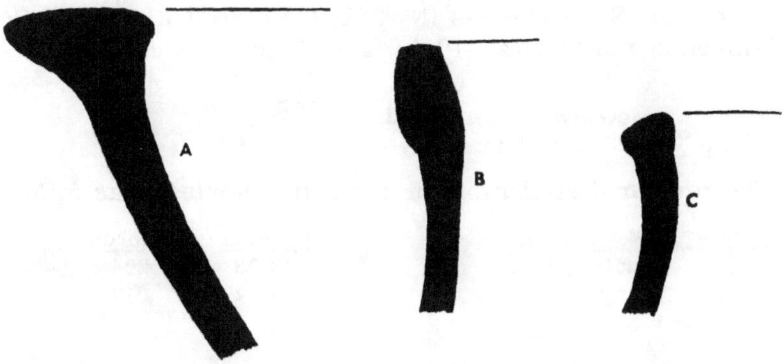

Fig. 17. Fort Ancient. (A) Brangenberg Plain; (B) Hopewell Rim; (C) McGraw Plain.

Hopewellian Series, Indeterminate Residue—1
Body sherds, Grit: 1 (unmeasurable)

Southeastern Series, Turner Simple-stamped *A*—12
Body sherds, Grit: 12 (4- 5 mm; 4.5 mm)

Southeastern Series, Turner Simple-stamped *B*—5
Body sherds, Sand: 5 (4- 5 mm; 4.5 mm)
(tetrapods: 4)

Southeastern Series, Untyped Cord-marked—14
Body sherds, Sand: 14 (7- 9 mm; 8.5 mm)

Total 313 sherds

Comments

The only noteworthy aspects of this material are in the Hopewellian and Southeastern Series. One of the Brangenberg rims clearly shows traces of red paint. The other Hopewellian Series sherds are all very crumbly. Rocker-stamping is very tight, at times almost "jabbed," and the cross-hatching on rims is shoddy. No interior grooves have been noted. Vessel size appears to be in the small to medium range.

The Untyped Cord-marked sherds of the Southeastern Series are somewhat thicker than usual; shapes could not be determined.

The distribution of the various ceramic series from Fort Ancient is as follows:

	Percent	Sherds
Scioto Series:	80.51	252
Hopewellian Series:	9.58	30
Southeastern Series:	9.90	31

Within the Scioto Series (N = 252) the distribution of McGraw Cord-marked and McGraw Plain is as follows:

	Percent	Sherds
McGraw Cord-marked:	83.33	210
McGraw Plain:	16.66	42

The temper distribution for the entire series is as follows:

	Percent	Sherds
Grit:	93.93	294
Sand:	6.07	19

FORT HILL

Fort Hill in Highland County, Ohio, is another of those large hilltop enclosures like Fort Ancient, which are presumed to be late on the Hopewell horizon. The fairly extensive body of literature on this site indicates that no artifacts whatsoever have been found within the enclosure. However, in the valley directly to the south, and at the foot of the "fort," two circular earthworks were excavated some years ago by R. S. Baby of the Ohio State Museum. These structures proved to be Hopewellian, and are presumed to be associated with the enclosure (Morgan and Thomas, 1948). In addition, during recent fieldwork which I carried out in 1964, several other small Hopewellian loci interpreted as farmsteads, were located at the foot of the hill. The ceramics here discussed were obtained during Baby's excavations; they are deposited in the Ohio State Museum under catalogue number 2189. The sherds were all associated with the circular structures which they should date.

Analysis

Scioto Series, McGraw Cord-marked—17
- Body sherds, Grit: 17 (4- 8 mm; 5.2 mm)

Scioto Series, McGraw Plain—124 (Fig. 18, A-E)
- Body sherds, Grit: 110 (4- 9 mm; 6.2 mm)
- Rim sherds, Grit: 14 (5- 8 mm; 6.5 mm)

Hopewellian Series, Chillicothe Brushed—10
- Body sherds, Grit: 10 (4- 5 mm; 4.5 mm)

Southeastern Series, Turner Simple-stamped *E*—1
- Body sherds, Sand: 1 (5 mm)

Southeastern Series, Untyped Plain—1 (Fig. 18, F)
- Rim sherds, Sand: 1 (4 mm)

Southeastern Series, Turner Check-stamped—1
Body sherds, Grit: 1 (4 mm)

Total 154 sherds

Comments

The majority of the sherds from Fort Hill are very crumbly. The Chillicothe Brushed sherds are very finely brushed. Vessels appear to have been small to medium in size.

The distribution of the various ceramic series from Fort Hill is as follows:

	Percent	Sherds
Scioto Series:	91.56	141
Hopewellian Series:	6.49	10
Southeastern Series:	1.94	3

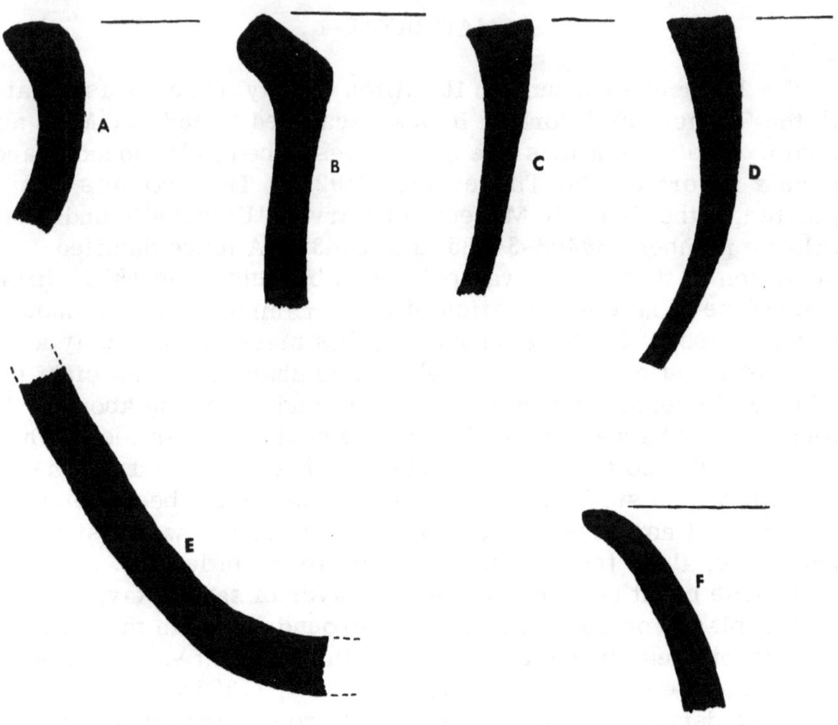

Fig. 18. Fort Hill. (A–E) McGraw Plain; (F) Southeastern Series, Untyped Plain.

Within the Scioto Series (N = 141) the distribution of McGraw Cord-marked and McGraw Plain is as follows:

	Percent	Sherds
McGraw Cord-marked:	12.05	17
McGraw Plain:	87.94	124

The temper distribution for the total series is as follows:

	Percent	Sherds
Grit:	98.70	152
Sand:	1.29	2

It should be noted that at a Hopewell site which from all other indications appears to be rather late, the reversal of the proportions of McGraw Cord-marked and McGraw Plain is curious. As a rule, cord-marked ware predominates on Middle and Late Hopewell sites.

MARRIOTT-1

The Marriott-1 mound in Hamilton County, Ohio, is associated with the Turner earthworks. It was excavated in 1884 by Metz and Putnam. The excavations are briefly described in Willoughby and Hooton's report on the Turner site (1922). The artifacts are deposited in the Peabody Museum of Harvard University under catalogue numbers 34408-34435, and 34437. A more detailed description of this mound was published by Putnam in 1886. It is of relevance to note the location of the ceramics within the mound. Putnam states: "Partly surrounding this mass of burnt clay was a mass of burnt earth, stones, ashes, and charcoal, from eight to ten inches in depth, irregular in outline, and extending about fifteen feet to the west, eight feet to the south, and ten feet to the east . . . . The bottom of this burnt material was about seven inches above the surface over which the mound had been made. About six feet northeast of the center of the mound was a similar burnt space, about ten feet in width and fifteen in length . . . . Under these burnt portions was a thin layer of sandy clay, which had been placed on the surface of the ground . . . . In the ashes and earth on these burnt areas, and in the adjacent earth, were over six hundred fragments of pottery . . . " (1886 *b*:451).

These data prove that the ceramics from Marriott-1 had originally been placed into the mound and were not part of the fill. Of the 600-plus sherds reported by Putnam, 448 could be traced in the Peabody Museum in 1964.

Analysis

Scioto Series, McGraw Cord-marked—255 (Fig. 19, A-E; Pl. 27, *b*)
- Body sherds, Grit: 169 (4-11 mm; 6.8 mm)
  - Limestone: 78 (4- 9 mm; 6.5 mm)
- Rim sherds, Grit: 3 (6-14 mm; 10.3 mm)
  - Limestone: 5 (5- 9 mm; 6.3 mm)

Scioto Series, McGraw Plain—122 (Fig. 19, F-K)
- Body sherds, Grit: 40 (4-10 mm; 6.5 mm)
  - Limestone: 64 (4-10 mm; 6.9 mm)
  - (lobed: 7)
- Rim sherds, Grit: 14 (4- 8 mm; 6.6 mm)
  - Limestone: 4 (5- 9 mm; 6.7 mm)

Hopewellian Series, Chillicothe Rocker-stamped—49
- A. Plain-rocked: 23 (Fig. 19, S; Pl. 28, *b*)
  - Body sherds, Grit: 13 (3- 7 mm; 5.0 mm)
    - Limestone: 7 (3- 7 mm; 5.2 mm)
    - (zoned: 9; lobed: 1)
  - Rim sherds, Grit: 2 (6.0 mm)
    - Limestone: 1 (5 mm)
- B. Plain long-rocked ("Pike"): 4 (Pl. 27, *e,f*)
  - Body sherds, Grit: 3 (3- 6 mm; 4.6 mm)
    - Limestone: 1 (4 mm)
- C. Dentate long-rocked ("Pike"): 2 (Pl. 27, *a,d*)
  - Body sherds, Grit: 2 (4- 5 mm; 4.5 mm)
- D. Dentate-rocked: 19 (Pl. 28, *c–d*)
  - Body sherds, Grit: 13 (4- 7 mm; 4.8 mm)
    - Limestone: 6 (4- 6 mm; 4.7 mm)
    - (zoned: 8)
- E. Plain and long-rocked mixed: 1
  - Body sherds, Limestone: 1 (4 mm)

Hopewellian Series, Chillicothe Brushed—2
- Body sherds, Grit: 2 (5.0 mm)
  - (zoned: 2)

Hopewellian Series, Chillicothe Incised—10 (Fig. 19, L-O, Q; Pl. 28, *a*)
- Body sherds, Grit: 1 (5 mm)
  - Limestone: 2 (4- 6 mm; 5.0 mm)
- Rim sherds, Grit: 6 (6- 7 mm; 6.5 mm)
  - Limestone: 1 (6 mm)

Hopewellian Series, Hopewell Rims—3 (Fig. 19, P, R; Pl. 27, *c*; Pl. 28, *e*)
- Grit: 2 (6.0 mm)
- Limestone: 1 (6 mm)

Hopewellian Series, Indeterminate Residue—5
- Body sherds, Grit: 4 (--)
  - Limestone: 1 (--)
  - (zoned: 5)

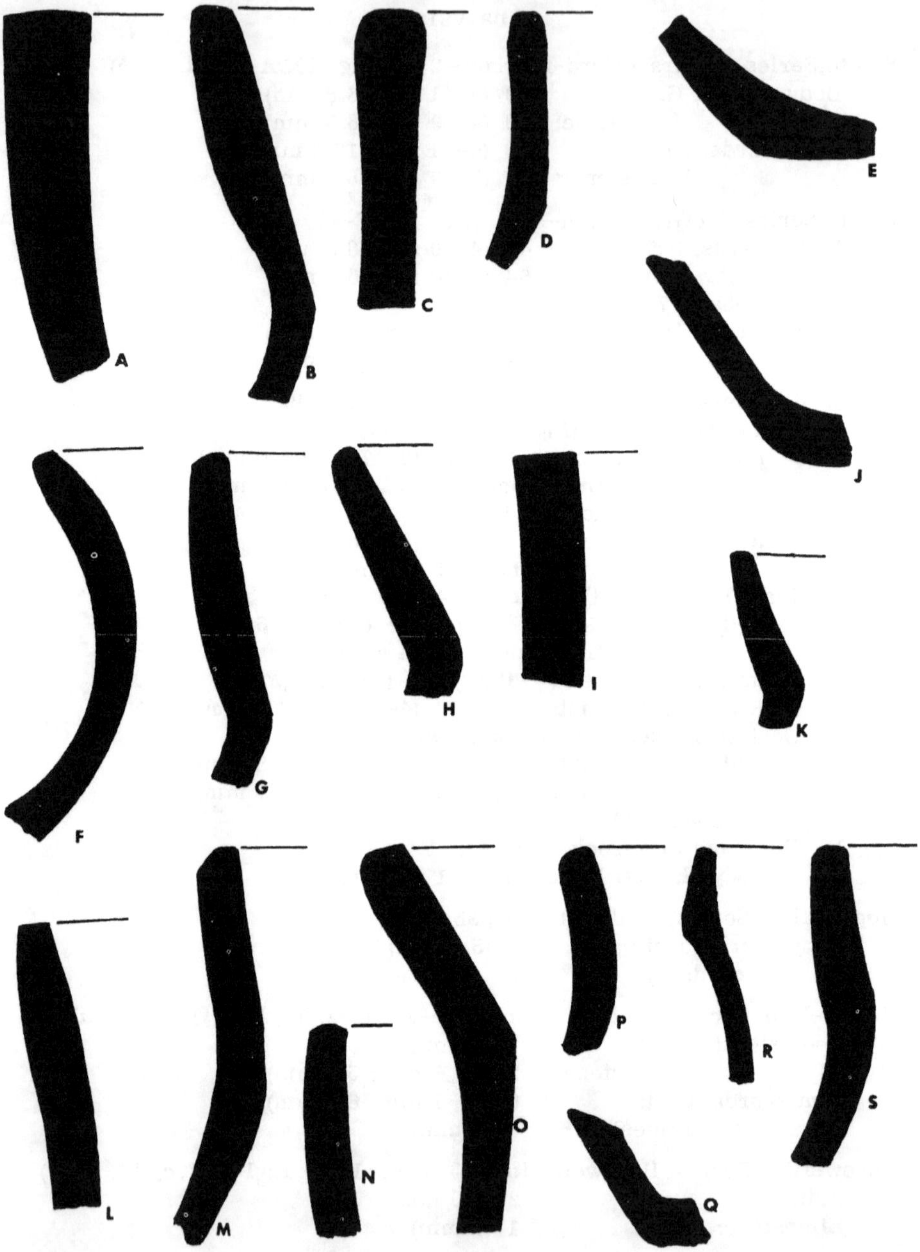

Fig. 19. (A-E) McGraw Cord-marked; (F-K) McGraw Plain; (L-O,Q) Chillicothe Incised; (P,R) Hopewell Rims; (S) Chillicothe Rocker-stamped, plain-rocked (on rim).

PLATE 27

Marriott-1. (*a,d*) Chillicothe Rocker-stamped, dentate long-rocked ("Pike"); (*b*) McGraw Cord-marked; (*c*) Hopewell Rim; (*e,f*) Chillicothe Rocker-stamped, plain long-rocked ("Pike").

PLATE 28

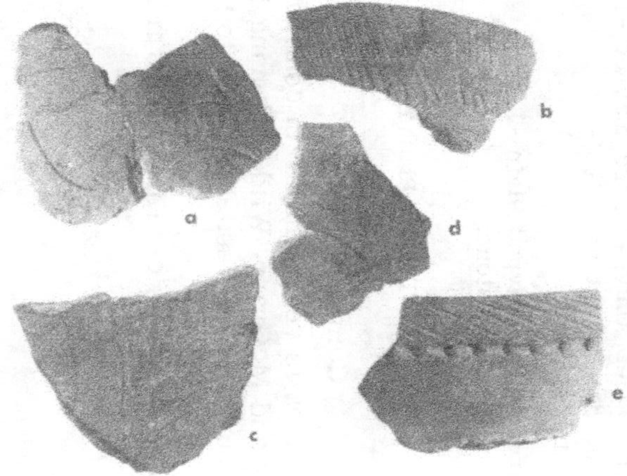

Marriott-1. (*a*) Chillicothe Incised; (*b*) Chillicothe Rocker-stamped, plain-rocked; (*c–d*) dentate-rocked; (*e*) Hopewell Rim.

Southeastern Series, Untyped Cord-marked—1
Body sherds, Limestone: 1 (--)
(tetrapodal)

Southeastern Series, Untyped Plain—1
Body sherds, Limestone: 1 (--)
(tetrapodal)

Total 448 sherds

Comments

The Hopewellian Series is very similar in configuration to its counterparts at Turner and McGraw. Wild rockering is quite common, fabrics are poor, and the vessels appear to have been quite large.

The distribution of the various ceramic series from Marriott-1 is as follows:

	Percent	Sherds
Scioto Series:	84.15	377
Hopewellian Series:	15.40	69
Southeastern Series:	.44	2

Within the Scioto Series (N = 377) the distribution of McGraw Cord-marked and McGraw Plain is as follows:

	Percent	Sherds
McGraw Cord-marked:	67.64	255
McGraw Plain:	32.36	122

The temper distribution for the total series is as follows:

	Percent	Sherds
Grit:	61.16	274
Limestone:	38.84	174

TURNER

The Turner site in Hamilton County, Ohio, was excavated by Putnam and his associates C. L. Metz, M. H. Saville, and E. Volk between 1882 and 1908 for the Peabody Museum of Harvard University. The finds from these operations, including the ceramics, are deposited *in toto* in the Peabody Museum. The final report on the site which includes a section on pottery, was published by Willoughby and Hooton (1922). In addition to the chapter on pottery (pp. 90-94) the text contains numerous references to ceramics and their provenience. Additional ceramic data are contained in S. F. Starr's study on the Archaeology of Hamilton County, Ohio (1960: 37-41).

Analysis: Turner-1

The report on this structure (Willoughby and Hooton, 1922: 28-32), and the Peabody catalogue contain numerous references to ceramics, some of which are highly specific. The following citations from the text are grouped in the order in which they will be presented below. Much of the material could be checked with the extant collections in the Peabody Museum and their references in the Museum catalogue.

Near the center of the mound the excavators found a presumed fire place, seven feet in diameter, which contained " . . . four pottery vessels . . . . Mixed with the ashes were charcoal, flint flakes, charred corn and corn-cobs" (Willoughby and Hooton, 1922: 29). This feature here constitutes Unit-1. In the Peabody catalogue it is referred to as the "refuse pile on north side" of the mound, and is covered by catalogue numbers 29571, 29571-A, 29572, and 29529-31. In the published report, three of the vessels are illustrated on Plate 22, *g-i*. Vessel *g*, a lobed bowl could not be traced in the collections and is, therefore, excluded from the count here; it is listed separately in the Appendix to the present discussion of the Turner site. Vessels *h* and *i* were studied. In this context it should be noted that vessel *i*, the curious zoned cord-marked pot, almost certainly is wrongly reconstructed; its shape would appear to have been quite different from that given in the illustration. Moreover, clearly more than one vessel was involved. The catalogue reference under numbers 29530-29531, referring to an "ashbed in center of mound at bottom" evidently designates the same feature.

In the southwestern portion of the mound an ashbed was encountered beneath a layer of carefully placed stones. This feature (here named Unit-2) can be equated with the catalogue number 29543, referring to provenience unit "on southwest side at bottom in ashes under layer of stones." According to the excavators this may in fact have been a cremation burial.

Two sherds in the collection bearing catalogue number A-636 were associated with "skeleton-1;" this is referred to in the site report as Grave 1; there is no mention of pottery in the text. This material here constitutes Unit-3.

Finally, seven sherds in the collection bearing catalogue number A-645 were found in an "ashbed 3 ft. 6 in. deep." This appears to be either of two layers marked 3 on the cross-section of the mound (Willoughby and Hooton, 1922:28-29, Fig. 12). This is here referred to as Unit-4.

Unit-5 refers to ceramics from the mound fill.

Unit-1: 29571, 29571-A, 29572, 29529-31

Scioto Series, McGraw Cord-marked—348 (Fig. 20, A–M; Pl. 29, *c*)
Body sherds, Grit: 21 (4- 8 mm; 5.8 mm)
Limestone: 296 (4-10 mm; 6.2 mm)
Rim sherds, Grit: 1 (4 mm)
Limestone: 28 (3-12 mm; 6.5 mm)
Vessels, Limestone: 2 (body: 8- 9 mm; rim: 6- 7 mm)

Scioto Series, McGraw Plain—14 (Fig. 21, N–P)
Body sherds, Grit: 1 (7 mm)
Limestone: 11 (4- 7 mm; 5.2 mm)
Rim sherds, Limestone: 2 (6- 8 mm; 7.0 mm)

Hopewellian Series, Chillicothe Rocker-stamped—9
B. Plain long-rocked ("Pike"): 2
Body sherds, Grit: 2 (4- 5 mm; 4.5 mm)
D. Dentate-rocked: 7 (Pl. 30, *a*)
Body sherds, Grit: 3 (4- 5 mm; 4.5 mm)
Limestone: 3 (4- 5 mm; 4.6 mm)
Vessel, Limestone: 1 (rim and body mean: 5.0 mm)
(zoned: 3)

Hopewellian Series, Chillicothe Brushed—1
Body sherds, Limestone: 1 (4 mm)
(zoned: 1)

Southeastern Series, Turner Check-stamped—1
Body sherds, Grit: 1 (5 mm)

Unknown Series, Zoned Cord-marked—7 (Fig. 21, Q–R; Pl. 33)
Body sherds, Grit: 2 (7.0 mm)
Mixed: 2 (7.0 mm)
Rim sherds, Grit: 2 (6.0 mm)
Limestone: 1 (5 mm)

Unknown Series, Exterior and Interior Cord-marked—1
Body sherds, Grit: 1 (6 mm)

Miami Series, Untyped Punctate—2
Body sherds, Grit: 1 (5 mm)
Limestone: 1 (4 mm)

Unknown Series, Zoned Grooved—1
Body sherds, Limestone: 1 (6 mm)

Total 384 sherds

Unit-2: 29543

Scioto Series, McGraw Cord-marked—1 (Fig. 20, N–O; Pl. 31, *a–c, g*)
Body sherds, Limestone: 1 (6 mm)

Unit-3: A-639

Scioto Series, McGraw Cord-marked—1
Body sherds, Limestone: 1 (6 mm)

Hopewellian Series, Seip Plain—1
Body sherds, Limestone: 1 (4 mm)
(lobed: 1)

Unit-4: A-645

Scioto Series, McGraw Cord-marked—7 (Pl. 29, *a–b*)
Body sherds, Limestone: 6 (4– 9 mm; 6.0 mm)
Rim sherds, Grit: 1 (5 mm)

Unit-5: Mound Fill

Scioto Series, McGraw Cord-marked—306 (Fig 21, A–G; Pl. 32, *d,e,h*)
Body sherds, Grit: 38 (4–10 mm; 5.2 mm)
Limestone: 242 (3–13 mm; 6.6 mm)
Rim sherds, Grit: 5 (5.0 mm)
Limestone: 21 (4–10 mm; 6.5 mm)

Scioto Series, McGraw Plain—69 (Fig. 21, H–M)
Body sherds, Grit: 21 (4– 8 mm; 5.6 mm)
Limestone: 24 (3– 9 mm; 6.1 mm)
Rim sherds, Grit: 14 (4– 7 mm; 5.1 mm)
Limestone: 10 (4–10 mm; 6.7 mm)

Hopewellian Series, Chillicothe Rocker-stamped—50
A. Plain-rocked—11 (Fig. 22, A–C; Pl. 31, *d*; Pl. 32, *i*)
Body sherds, Grit: 5 (4– 5 mm; 4.8 mm)
Limestone: 5 (4– 5 mm; 4.6 mm)
(zoned: 4)
Rim sherds, Grit: 1 (4 mm)
B. Plain long-rocked ("Pike")—24 (Pl. 31, *f*; Pl. 32, *a,c,f,g,j*)
Body sherds, Grit: 11 (4– 7 mm; 5.2 mm)
Limestone: 13 (3– 7 mm; 4.5 mm)
C. Dentate long-rocked ("Pike")—10 (Pl. 32, *a*)
Body sherds, Grit: 7 (3– 7 mm; 4.7 mm)
Limestone: 3 (3– 6 mm; 5.6 mm)
(zoned: 2)
D. Dentate-rocked—5 (Pl. 32, *i*)
Body sherds, Limestone: 4 (3– 7 mm; 5.0 mm)
(zoned: 3)
Rim sherds, Grit: 1 (4 mm)

Hopewellian Series, Hopewell Rims—2 (Fig. 22, D; Pl. 31, *e*)
Grit: 2 (5.0 mm)

Southeastern Series, Turner Simple-stamped *B*—2
Body sherds, Sand: 2 (5.0 mm)

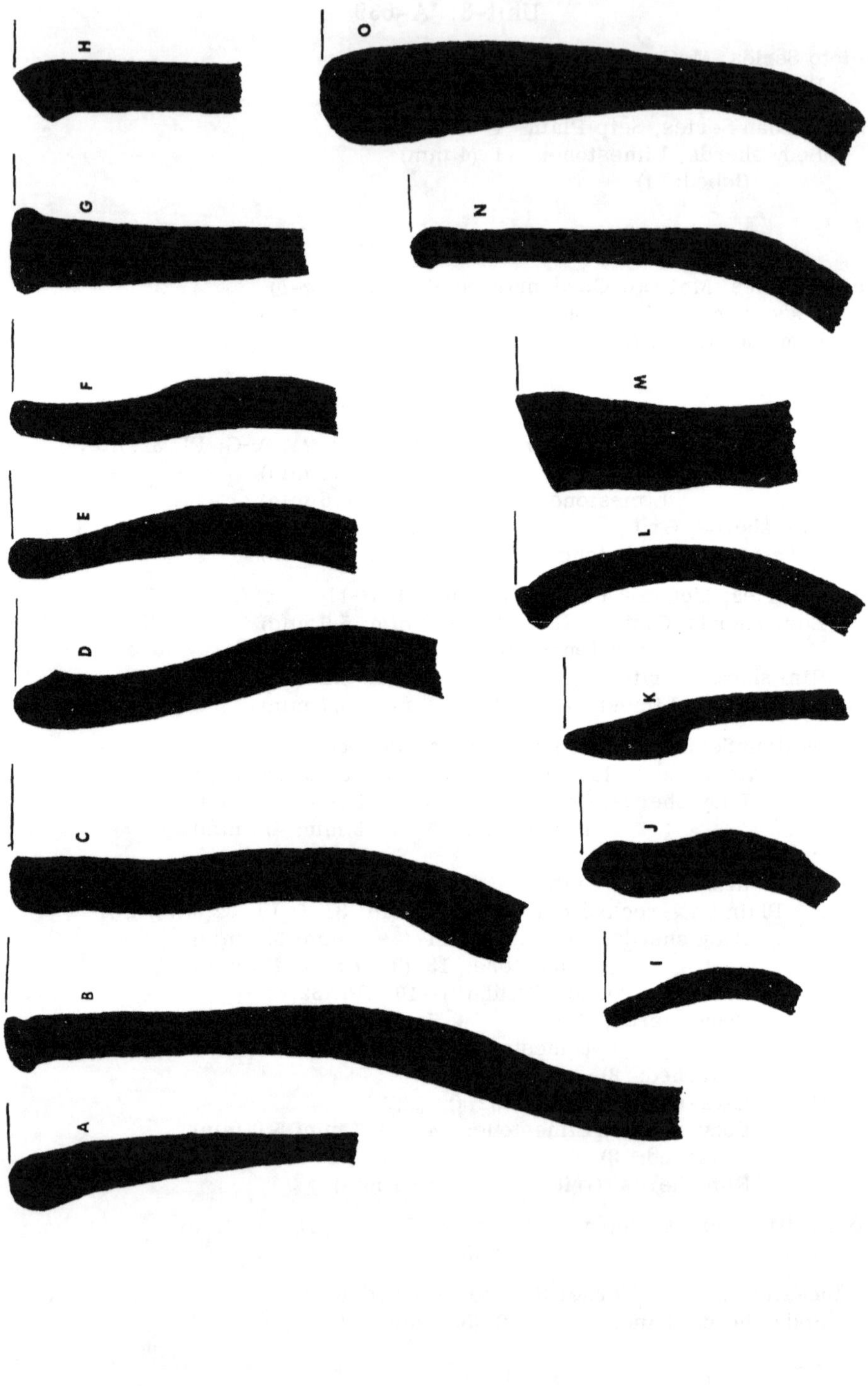

Fig. 20. Turner-1. (A–M = unit-1) McGraw Cord-marked; (N–O = unit-2).

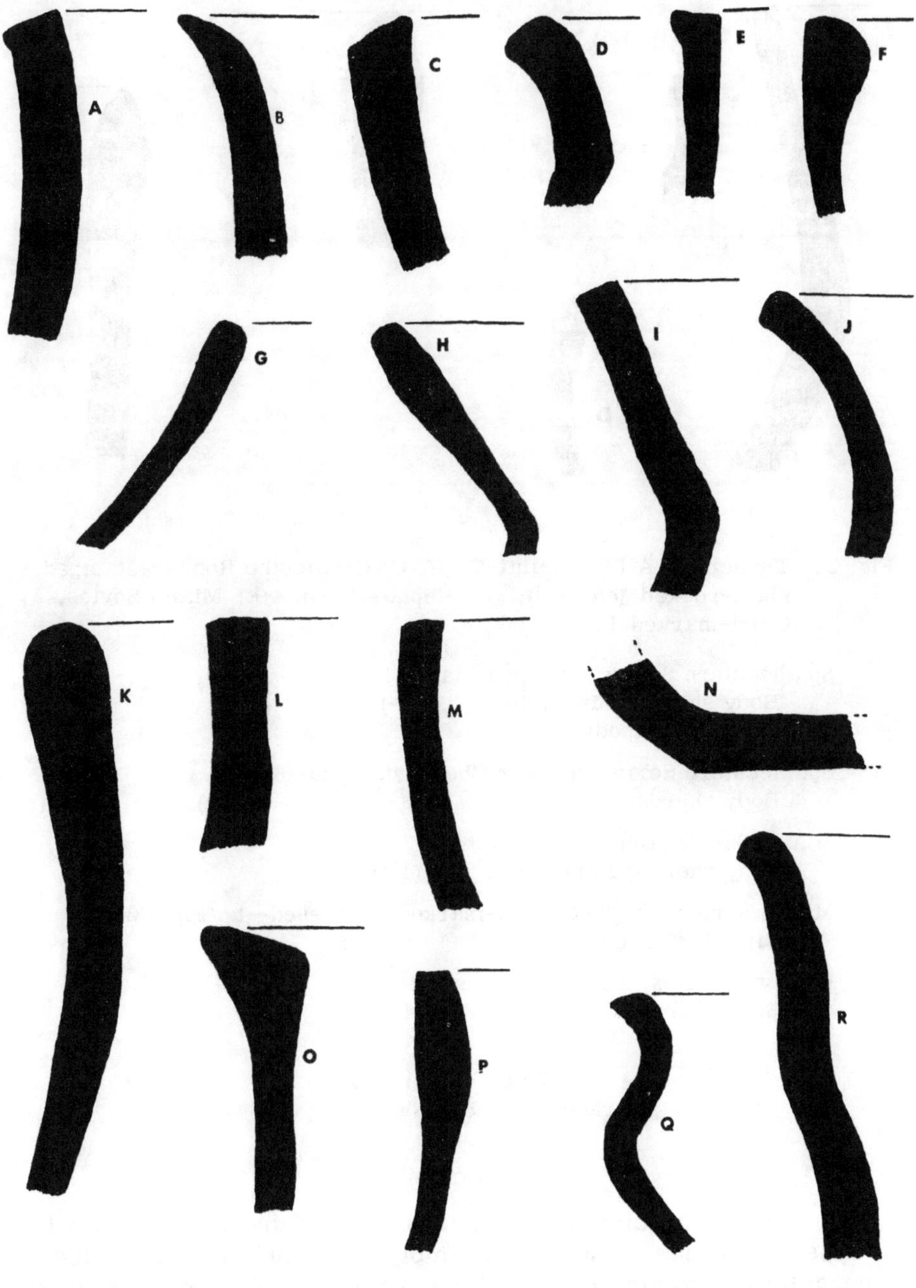

Fig. 21. Turner-1. (A-G = unit 5) McGraw Cord-marked; (H-M = unit-5) McGraw Plain; (N-P = unit-1) McGraw Plain; (Q-R = unit-1) Cord-marked Zoned.

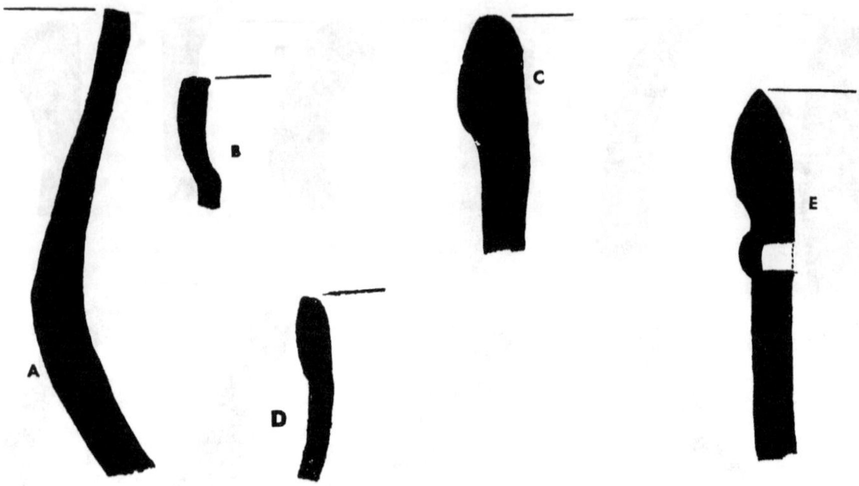

Fig. 22. Turner-1. All from unit-5. (A-C) Chillicothe Rocker-stamped, plain-rocked (on rim); (D) Hopewell Rim; (E) Miami Series, Cord-marked Embossed.

Southeastern Series, Untyped Plain—1
Body sherds, Limestone: 1 (--)
(tetrapod)

Southeastern Series, Turner Check-stamped—6
Body sherds, Limestone: 6 (3- 5 mm; 4.8 mm)

Miami Series, Untyped Punctate—1
Body sherds, Limestone: 1 (4 mm)

Miami Series, Untyped Cord-marked Embossed—1 (Fig. 22, E)
Rim sherds, Grit: 1 (8 mm)

Unknown Series, Zoned Cord-marked—2
Body sherds, Grit: 1 (4 mm)
Limestone: 1 (4 mm)

Total 440 sherds
Grand Total 834 sherds

Comments

The abundant Scioto Series sherds from Turner-1 conform to the type definitions. They are crumbly and poorly fired, and there is considerable variability in temper particle size. Of interest is a cord-marked rim sherd with a thickened rim strip similar to that of some classic Hopewell rims.

PLATE 29

Turner-1. (*a–b* = unit-4) McGraw Cord-marked; (*c* = unit-1) McGraw Cord-marked.

PLATE 30

Turner-1. (*a* = unit-1) Chillicothe Rocker-stamped, dentate-rocked. Photograph by Peabody Museum, Harvard University.)

PLATE 31

Turner-1. (*a–c,g*) McGraw Cord-marked; (*d*) Chillicothe Rocker-stamped, plain-rocked; (*e*) Hopewell Rim; (*f*) Chillicothe Rocker-stamped, plain long-rocked ("Pike").

PLATE 32

Turner-1. All unit-5. (*a,c,f,g,j*) Chillicothe Rocker-stamped, plain long-rocked ("Pike"); (*b*) dentate rocked; (*i*) plain rocked; (*d,e,h*) McGraw cord-marked.

PLATE 33

Turner-1. (*a* = unit-1) Unknown Series, Zoned Cord-marked.

PLATE 34

Turner-3. All unit-4. (*a,c*) Turner Simple-stamped *B*; (*b,d*) McGraw Cord-marked.

The sherds in the Hopewellian Series are characterized, in the main, by poorly fired fabrics, shoddily applied decorations, very little polishing, and great variability in rim shape. In addition to some classic Hopewell Rims, supposed later forms with deep interior grooving occur, and, most commonly, more or less pronouncedly everted or flaring rims.

Of considerable interest are the curious zoned cord-marked sherds which have only been noted at Turner-1, Turner-3, and in the material from the Turner Embankment. They defy classification. The zoning here consists of deeply incised, wide, curvilinear lines on the upper body. These delineate cord-marked areas.

The sherds in the provisional Miami Series seem to be similar to Weaver ware in Illinois. The thick interiorally and exteriorally cord-marked sherd has its counterparts at Turner-6 and in the Turner Cemetary area. The zoned-grooved rim sherd appears to represent a bowl with horizontal incised grooves, placed at regular intervals of less than one cm around the vessel, starting just below the rim.

The distribution of the various ceramic series from Turner-1 is as follows:

	Percent	Sherds
Scioto Series:	89.44	747
Hopewellian Series:	7.55	63
Southeastern Series:	1.20	10
Miami Series:	.48	4
Other:	1.32	11

Within the Scioto Series (N = 747) the distribution of McGraw Cord-marked and McGraw Plain is as follows:

	Percent	Sherds
McGraw Cord-marked:	88.88	663
McGraw Plain:	11.12	83

The temper distribution for the total series is as follows:

	Percent	Sherds
Grit:	17.14	143
Limestone:	82.37	687
Sand:	.24	2
Mixed:	.24	2

Analysis: Turner-3

This mound is discussed in Willoughby and Hooton (1922:33-62). It was one of the most spectacular structures of the entire site. Available provenience data on ceramics are derived from this report and from the Peabody Museum catalogue notations.

The following is a summary of the catalogue data which will subsequently be equated with the published report:

Nos. 30052-30053, 30058—ashpit under mound
Nos. 30034-30036—ashpit in center of mound
No. 34721—altar west of central altar
Nos. 34831-34851, 34853—general diggings.

The published data on ceramics from Turner-3 are exceedingly scanty. It is of relevance to mention here that there were found diverse submound features underlying the "concrete" floor of the structure. In terms of ceramic finds the following quotation from Metz' notes should be given: "Just beneath the layer of concrete or burned gravel, a heavy stratum of earth was observed. This was carefully uncovered and proved to be a hearth of semicircular form, conforming lengthwise to the curve of the mound . . . . The surface was burned to a hard red brick, 3 to 4 inches in depth, beneath which was a layer of black ashes, 3 inches in depth" (Willoughby and Hooton, 1922:37). It may safely be assumed that the ceramics catalogued under numbers 30052-53, and 30058 came from these areas.

Unit-1: 30052-53, 30058

Scioto Series, McGraw Cord-marked—5 (Fig. 23, D)
Body sherds, Grit: 2 (7- 9 mm; 7.6 mm)
Limestone: 1 (7 mm)
Rim sherds, Limestone: 2 (6.0 mm)

Scioto Series, McGraw Plain—2
Body sherds, Grit: 2 (5- 7 mm; 6.0 mm)

Unknown Series, Untyped Fabric-impressed—2
Body sherds, Grit: 1 (8 mm)
Rim sherds, Grit: 1 (5 mm)

Total 9 sherds

Unit-2: 30034-36

Scioto Series, McGraw Cord-marked—22
Body sherds, Grit: 6 (5- 7 mm; 6.0 mm)
Limestone: 16 (3- 9 mm; 5.0 mm)

Scioto Series, McGraw Plain—11 (Fig. 23, I)
Body sherds, Grit: 10 (3- 7 mm; 4.9 mm)
Rim sherds, Grit: 1 (6 mm)

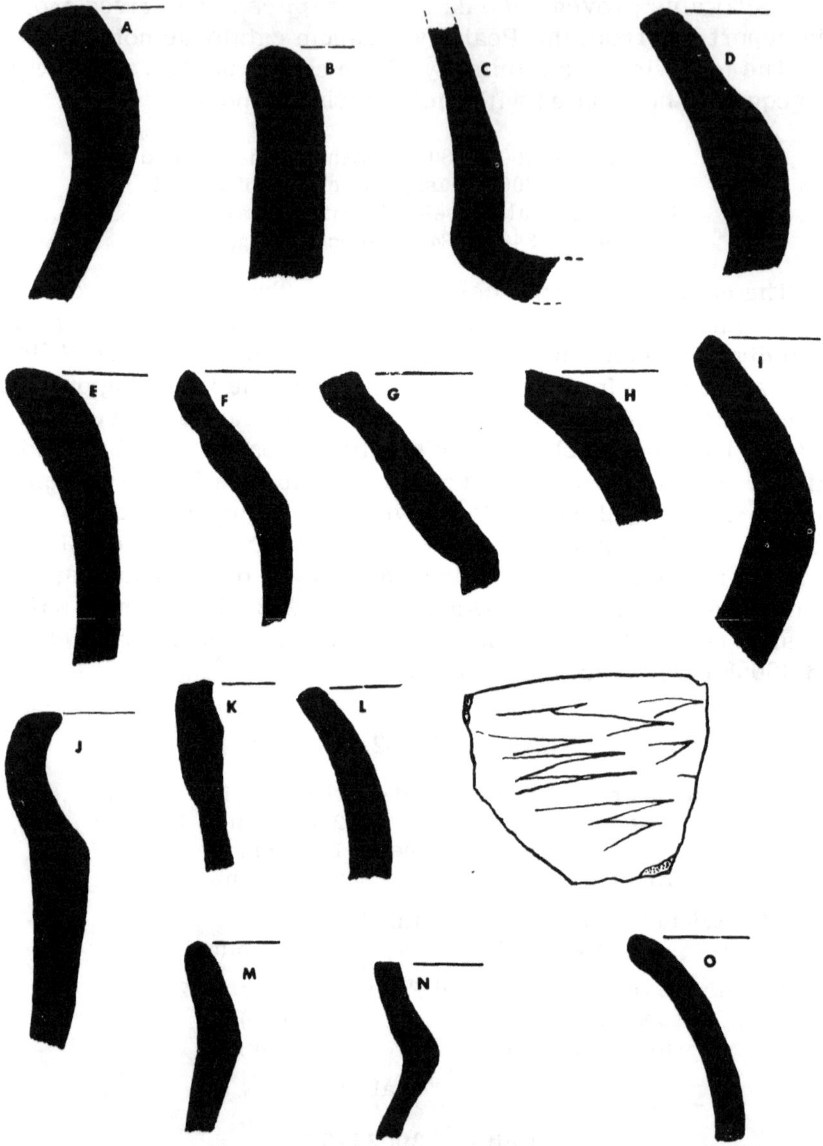

Fig. 23. Turner-3. (A-C = unit-4) McGraw Cord-marked; (D = unit-1) McGraw Cord-marked; (E-H = unit-4) McGraw Plain; (I = unit-2) McGraw Plain; (J = unit-2) Chillicothe Rocker-stamped, plain long-rocked ("Pike") (on rim); (K-L = unit-4) plain-rocked (on rim); (M-N = unit-4) Hopewell Rims; (0 = unit-4) Turner Simple-stamped *B*.

Hopewellian Series, Chillicothe Rocker-stamped—6
A. Plain-rocked: 3
Body sherds, Limestone: 2 (5- 6 mm; 5.5 mm)
Rim sherds, Limestone: 1 (5 mm)
B. Plain long-rocked ("Pike"): 1 (Fig. 23, J)
Body sherds, Grit: 1 (5 mm)
D. Dentate-rocked: 2
Body sherds; Grit: 2 (4.0 mm)

Hopewellian Series, Indeterminate Residue—2
Body sherds, Grit: 2 (5- 6 mm; 5.5 mm)

Southeastern Series, Turner Simple-stamped *B*—2
Body sherds, Sand: 2 (5.0 mm)
(tetrapods: 2)

Southeastern Series, Turner Check-stamped—1
Body sherds, Limestone: 1 (5 mm)

Total 44 sherds

Unit-3: 34721

Scioto Series, McGraw Cord-marked—5
Body sherds, Grit: 5 (5- 6 mm; 5.8 mm)

Unit-4: Mound Fill

Scioto Series, McGraw Cord-marked—332 (Fig. 23, A-C; Pl. 34, *b,d;* Pl. 35, *a–d*)
Body sherds, Grit: 165 (3-12 mm; 5.4 mm)
Limestone: 160 (3-11 mm; 6.0 mm)
Rim sherds, Limestone: 5 (5- 9 mm; 7.3 mm)
Mixed: 2 (4- 8 mm; 6.0 mm)

Scioto Series, McGraw Plain—145 (Fig. 23, E-H)
Body sherds, Grit: 33 (4-13 mm; 7.0 mm)
Limestone: 90 (3-11 mm; 6.6 mm)
Rim sherds, Grit: 8 (7-10 mm; 8.0 mm)
Limestone: 14 (7-10 mm; 8.4 mm)

Hopewellian Series, Chillicothe Rocker-stamped—45
A. Plain-rocked: 3 (Fig. 23, K-L)
Body sherds, Limestone: 3 (4- 6 mm; 5.3 mm)
B. Plain long-rocked ("Pike"): 24 (Pl. 36, *b–c*)
Body sherds, Grit: 9 (4- 5 mm; 5.5 mm)
Limestone: 14 (3- 7 mm; 5.0 mm)
Mixed: 1 (5 mm)
(zoned: 1)
D. Dentate-rocked: 18
Body sherds, Grit: 10 (3- 8 mm; 5.0 mm)
Limestone: 4 (3- 5 mm; 4.0 mm)
Mixed: 3 (5- 6 mm; 5.0 mm)

PLATE 35

Turner-3. (*a–d* = unit-4) McGraw Cord-marked.

PLATE 36

Turner-3. All unit-4. (*a*) Untyped Fabric-impressed; (*b–c*) Chillicothe Rocker-stamped, plain long-rocked ("Pike").

(zoned: 6)
Rim sherds, Grit: 1 (4 mm)

Hopewellian Series, Chillicothe Brushed—2
Body sherds, Limestone: 1 (4 mm)
(zoned: 1)
Rim sherds, Limestone: 1 (5 mm)

Hopewellian Series, Chillicothe Incised—2
Body sherds, Grit: 2 (3- 5 mm; 4.0 mm)

Hopewellian Series, Untyped Zoned Incised—7
Body sherds, Mixed: 6 (2- 5 mm; 3.5 mm)
Rim sherds, Limestone: 1 (5 mm)

Hopewellian Series, Hopewell Rims—5 (Fig. 23, M-N)
Grit: 1 (4 mm)
Limestone: 2 (3- 4 mm; 3.5 mm)
Mixed: 2 (4- 5 mm; 4.5 mm)

Southeastern Series, Turner Simple-stamped *A*—2
Body sherds, Grit: 1 (--)
(tetrapod: 1)
Limestone: 1 (4 mm)

Southeastern Series, Turner Simple-stamped *B*—15 (Fig. 23, O; Pl. 34, *a*,*c*)
Body sherds, Sand: 12 (4- 6 mm; 5.5 mm)
Rim sherds, Sand: 3 (4- 5 mm; 4.3 mm)

Southeastern Series, Untyped Plain—2
Body sherds, Limestone: 1 (--)
(tetrapod: 1)
Sand: 1 (4 mm)

Southeastern Series, Untyped Cord-marked—4
Body sherds, Grit: 2 (--)
Limestone: 2 (--)
(tetrapods: 4)

Unknown Series, Cord-marked Zoned—2
Body sherds, Grit: 2 (7.0 mm)

Unknown Series, Untyped Fabric-impressed—2 (Pl. 36, *a*)
Body sherds, Sandy Grit: 2 (7.0 mm)

Miami Series, Untyped Punctate—1 (Pl. 37, *a*)
Body sherds, Grit: 1 (5 mm)

Total 564 sherds
Grand Total 624 sherds

Comments

All comments made under Turner-1 apply to this mound as well. The distribution of the various ceramic series at Turner-3 is as follows:

	Percent	Sherds
Scioto Series:	83.65	522
Hopewellian Series:	11.06	69
Southeastern Series:	4.16	26
Miami Series:	0.16	1
Other:	.96	6

Within the Scioto Series (N = 521) the distribution of McGraw Cord-marked and McGraw Plain is as follows:

	Percent	Sherds
McGraw Cord-marked:	69.73	364
McGraw Plain:	30.26	158

The temper distribution for the total series is as follows:

	Percent	Sherds
Grit:	43.27	270
Limestone:	51.60	322
Sand:	2.88	18
Mixed:	2.24	14

Analysis: Turner-4

This mound is discussed in the Turner report by Willoughby and Hooton (1922:62-74). There is not a single reference to ceramics in the relevant section of the report. In the chapter on pottery (Willoughby and Hooton, 1922:90-94), there are two brief statements regarding pottery from Turner-4. The first of these consists of two illustrations (Plate 22, *a*, *e*) representing two reconstructed vessels from the "general diggings;" one of these appears to have been a Brangenberg Plain vessel. The second reference, on page 93, merely states that the mound yielded a number of tetrapodal supports.

The Peabody Museum catalogue data are not much more revealing. The only specific reference to a feature associated with pottery is a notation with catalogue number 34620 which states that the sherds here were found in "pit No. 1, large pit under mound." For the remaining numbers the data either explicitly or implicitly suggest a mound fill or "general diggings" provenience.

The particular pit mentioned in the catalogue can not be traced on the mound plan or in the descriptive sections of the site report; the reason for this may be contained in this statement: "Thirteen pits and one hundred and seven post-holes, not shown in the ground plan, figure 28, are recorded. As it is not possible to plot these with accuracy from the given data they are omitted" (Willoughby and Hooton, 1922:62-63).

PLATE 37

Turner-3. (*a* = unit-4) Miami Series, Punctate.

PLATE 38

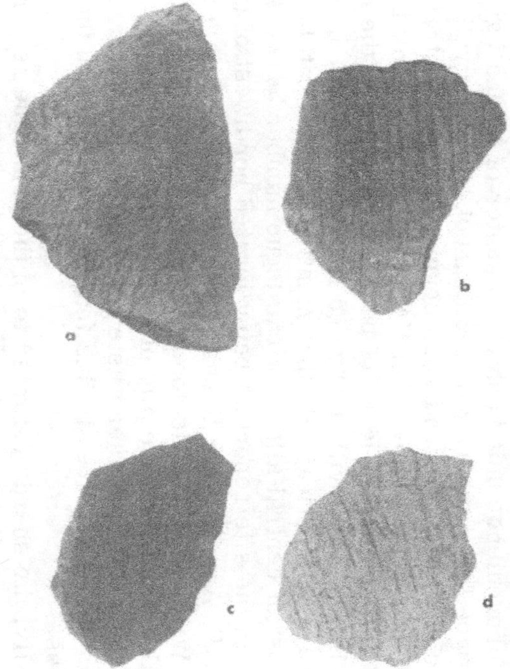

Turner-4. (*a–d* = all unit-2) McGraw Cord-marked.

It should be noted that the materials for several catalogue numbers referring to ceramics could not be traced in the collections.

The provenience unit "ash pit in center of mound" given in the catalogue for numbers 30034-36 cannot be traced with certainty. The center of the mound was occupied by the "central altar." The published report states that "About 10 inches below the floor of the altar was another layer of burnt clay, probably the remains of an earlier altar" (Willoughby and Hooton, 1922:45). Possibly this is the unit identical with that mentioned in the catalogue. The "altar west of central altar" of catalogue number 34721 is referred to in the site report as being located northwest of the "central altar." Among other things it was found to contain a few potsherds. Willoughby and Hooton further state that "North of the central altar was a refuse pile of ashes mixed with broken animal bones, potsherds, and other waste material" (1922:45). No ceramics that could be ascribed to this feature were found in the Museum collections.

Finally, the sherds referred to in the catalogue as derived from the "general diggings" presumably constitute mound fill material.

Examination of the evidence of Turner-4 permits this statement: It is possible to distinguish, on the basis of provenience units, three groups of sherds of possible chronological significance. In the presumed order of chronological deposition they are:

a. Sherds that may antedate the construction of the mound, being located in submound features.

b. Sherds from mound features deposited during the "operational" phase of the mound.

c. Sherds from mound fill which may either have been scooped up with the fill dirt representing premound materials, or similarly scooped up sherds representing material used and broken during the construction of the mound.

Comparison of the three ceramic groups shows no appreciable difference between the component sherds. This suggests essential contemporaneity of all the material.

Unit-1: 34620

Scioto Series, McGraw Cord-marked—4

Body sherds,	Grit:	1 (5 mm)
	Limestone:	3 (4- 5 mm; 4.3 mm)

Unit-2: Mound Fill

Scioto Series, McGraw Cord-marked—260 (Fig. 24, A-G; Pl. 38, *a-d*)
Body sherds, Grit: 176 (3-10 mm; 5.0 mm)
Limestone: 73 (3-10 mm; 5.9 mm)
Rim sherds, Grit: 7 (4- 9 mm; 5.8 mm)
Limestone: 4 (6-11 mm; 8.6 mm)

Scioto Series, McGraw Plain—144 (Fig. 24, H-P)
Body sherds, Grit: 36 (4- 9 mm; 5.8 mm)
Limestone: 73 (4-10 mm; 6.7 mm)
Mixed: 1 (9 mm)
Rim sherds, Grit: 20 (6- 9 mm; 7.2 mm)
Limestone: 14 (5-10 mm; 8.0 mm)

Hopewellian Series, Chillicothe Rocker-stamped—74
A. Plain-rocked: 14 (Fig. 25, D; Pl. 39, *b,c*)
Body sherds, Grit: 8 (3- 7 mm; 5.0 mm)
Limestone: 5 (3- 7 mm; 4.6 mm)
(zoned: 5)
Rim sherds, Limestone: 1 (4 mm)
B. Plain long-rocked ("Pike"): 32 (Pl. 39, *d,e*)
Body sherds, Grit: 16 (4- 8 mm; 4.9 mm)
Limestone: 11 (3- 8 mm; 3.8 mm)
(zoned: 2)
Rim sherds, Grit: 4 (4- 6 mm; 5.0 mm)
Limestone: 1 (5 mm)
D. Dentate-rocked: 28
Body sherds, Grit: 19 (3- 6 mm; 4.5 mm)
Limestone: 4 (3- 6 mm; 4.2 mm)
Mixed: 3 (4- 5 mm; 4.6 mm)
(zoned: 3)
Rim sherds, Grit: 2 (5.0 mm)

Hopewellian Series, Chillicothe Brushed—1
Rim sherds, Limestone: 1 (4 mm)

Hopewellian Series, Chillicothe Incised—4 (Fig. 25, B-C)
Rim sherds, Grit: 1 (4 mm)
Limestone: 3 (5- 7 mm; 6.3 mm)

Hopewellian Series, Untyped Dentate-stamped—1 (Pl. 39, *a*)
Body sherds, Grit: 1 (6 mm)

Hopewellian Series, Brangenberg Plain—2 (Fig. 25, A)
Rim sherds, Grit: 2 (10.0 mm)

Hopewellian Series, Hopewell Rims—9 (Fig. 25, E-F)
Grit: 3 (5.0 mm)
Limestone: 6 (4- 8 mm; 6.0 mm)

Hopewellian Series, Indeterminate Residue—7
Body sherds, Grit: 3 (--)

PLATE 39

Turner-4. All unit-2. (*a*) Hopewellian Series. Untyped Dentate-stamped; (*b–c*) Chillicothe Rocker-stamped, plain long-rocked ("Pike"); (*d–e*) plain-rocked.

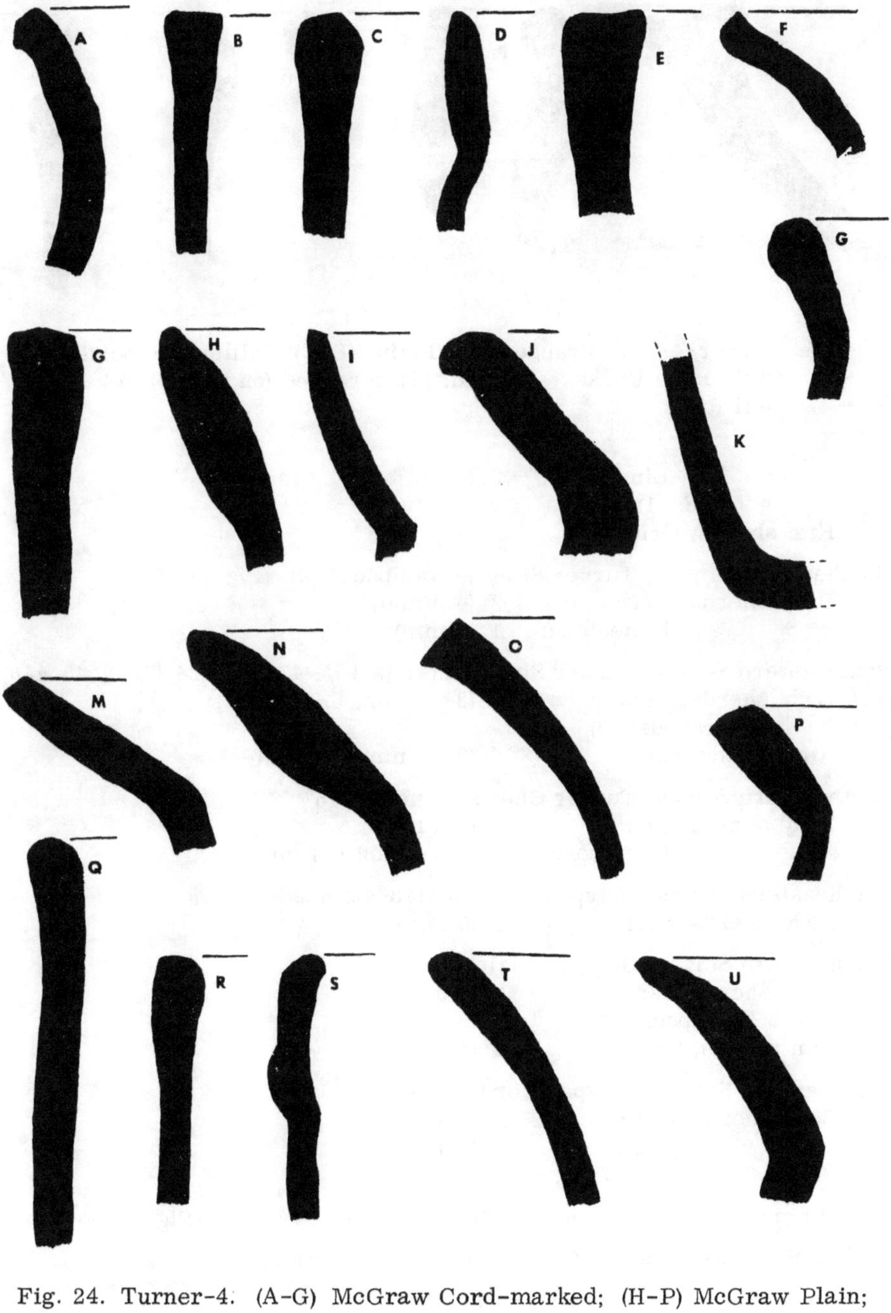

Fig. 24. Turner-4. (A-G) McGraw Cord-marked; (H-P) McGraw Plain; (Q-S) Miami Series, Punctate; (T) Turner Simple-stamped *B*; (U) Turner Simple-stamped *A*.

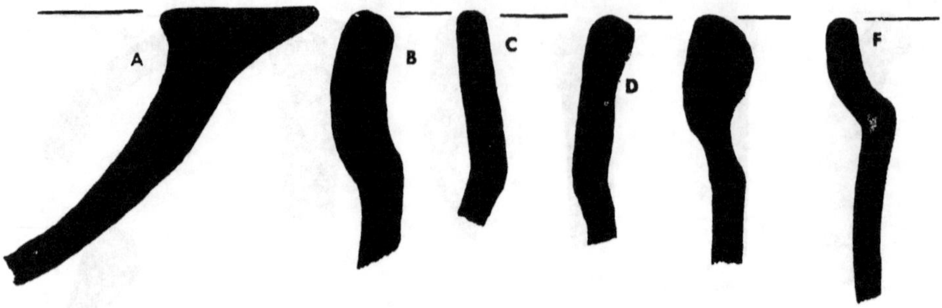

Fig. 25. Turner-4. (A) Brangenberg Plain; (B–C) Chillicothe Incised; (D) Chillicothe Rocker-stamped, plain-rocked (on rim); (E–F) Hopewell Rims.

Limestone: 3 (4- 6 mm; 4.6 mm)
(lobed: 1)
Rim sherds, Grit: 1 (--)

Southeastern Series, Turner Simple-stamped *A*—3 (Fig. 24, U)
Body sherds, Grit: 2 (4.0 mm)
Limestone: 1 (5 mm)

Southeastern Series, Turner Simple-stamped *B*—47 (Fig. 24, T; Pl. 40, *a–b*)
Body sherds, Sand: 43 (3- 9 mm; 5.0 mm)
(tetrapods: 3)
Rim sherds, Sand: 4 (3- 6 mm; 4.2 mm)

Southeastern Series, Turner Check-stamped—15
Body sherds, Grit: 2 (6.0 mm)
Limestone: 13 (5-11 mm; 6.4 mm)

Southeastern Series, Untyped Complicated-stamped—1
Body sherds, Grit: 1 (9 mm)

Southeastern Series, Untyped Plain—4
Body sherds, Sand: 3 (6.0 mm)
(tetrapods: 2)
Rim sherds, Sand: 1 (5 mm)

Southeastern Series, Untyped Cord-marked—7
Body sherds, Grit: 6 (--)
Sand: 1 (--)
(tetrapods: 7)

Miami Series, Untyped Punctate (2) and Embossed (1)—3 (Fig. 24, Q-S)
Rim sherds, Grit: 3 (5- 7 mm; 6.0 mm)

Total 582 sherds
Grand Total 586 sherds

PLATE 40

Turner-4. (*a*–*b* = unit-2) Turner Simple-stamped *B*

PLATE 41

Turner-6. (*a*) McGraw Cord-marked.

Comments

In general the same comments made for Turner-1 and Turner-3 hold true for this mound as well. In the Hopewellian Series, the Chillicothe Incised sherds have rim decorations (diagonal incised lines) similar to those found on McGraw material (Prufer and McKenzie, 1965). Among the Hopewell Rims interior grooving is conspicuous. The Complicated-stamped sherd is similar to those from Seip-2.

The distribution of the various ceramic series from Turner-4 is as follows:

	Percent	Sherds
Scioto Series:	69.62	408
Hopewellian Series:	16.72	98
Southeastern Series:	13.14	77
Miami Series:	.51	3

Within the Scioto Series (N = 408 sherds) the distribution of McGraw Cord-marked and McGraw Plain is as follows:

	Percent	Sherds
McGraw Cord-marked:	64.70	264
McGraw Plain:	35.27	144

The temper distribution for the total series is as follows:

	Percent	Sherds
Grit:	53.58	314
Limestone:	36.86	216
Sand:	8.87	52
Mixed:	.86	4

Analysis: Turner-6

There is no reference in the published report on this structure that might indicate the presence of ceramics (Willoughby and Hooton, 1922:75-76). The Peabody Museum collections, under numbers 34495-98, have listed, however, a number of sherds from this mound; they were recovered from the "general diggings."

Scioto Series, McGraw Cord-marked—27 (Fig. 26, J, K; Pl. 41, *a*)

Body sherds, Grit:	6	(4- 9 mm; 7.0 mm)
Limestone:	20	(3- 8 mm; 5.2 mm)
Rim sherds, Grit:	1	(12 mm)

Scioto Series, McGraw Plain—10 (Fig. 26, L-M)

Body sherds, Grit:	2	(5- 6 mm; 5.5 mm)
Limestone:	6	(5- 8 mm; 5.6 mm)

Fig. 26. Turner-7. (A) Chillicothe Rocker-Stamped, plain-rocked (on rim). Turner-9 (B-C) McGraw Plain; (D) Chillicothe Rocker-Stamped, dentate long-rocked ("Pike"). Turner Cemetery. (E = unit-6) McGraw Cord-marked; (F = unit-1) McGraw Plain; (G = unit-6) Southeastern Series, Untyped Plain; (H = unit-6) Chillicothe Rocker-Stamped, plain long-rocked ("Pike"); (I = unit 6) Unknown Series, Incised-grooved. Turner-6. (J-K) McGraw Cord-marked; (L-M) McGraw Plain; (N) Chillicothe Rocker-stamped, plain long-rocked ("Pike") (on rim); (L) Chillicothe Incised; (P) Chillicothe Brushed.

Rim sherds, Grit: 1 (7 mm)
Limestone: 1 (11 mm)

Hopewellian Series, Chillicothe Rocker-stamped—6
A. Plain-rocked: 4
Body sherds, Limestone: 3 (2.0 mm)
(zoned: 3)
Rim sherds, Grit: 1 (4 mm)
B. Plain long-rocked ("Pike"): 1 (Fig. 26, N)
Body sherds, Grit: 1 (5 mm)
(zoned: 1)
D. Dentate-rocked: 1
Rim sherds, Grit: 1 (3 mm)

Hopewellian Series, Chillicothe Brushed—1 (Fig. 26, P)
Rim sherds, Grit: 1 (4 mm)

Hopewellian Series, Chillicothe Incised—1 (Fig. 26, O)
Rim sherds, Grit: 1 (5 mm)

Southeastern Series, Turner Simple-stamped *A*—3
Body sherds, Grit: 3 (5- 8 mm; 6.6 mm)

Unknown Series, Exterior and Interior Cord-marked—1
Rim sherds, Grit: 1 (9 mm)

Total 49 sherds

Comments

The comments made under Turner-1 hold for this mound as well. The distribution of the various ceramic series from Turner-6 is as follows:

	Percent	Sherds
Scioto Series:	75.51	37
Hopewellian Series:	16.32	8
Southeastern Series:	6.12	3
Other:	2.04	1

Within the Scioto Series (N = 37) the distribution of McGraw Cord-marked and McGraw Plain is as follows:

	Percent	Sherds
McGraw Cord-marked:	73.00	27
McGraw Plain:	27.00	10

The temper distribution for the total series is as follows:

	Percent	Sherds
Grit:	38.77	19
Limestone:	61.22	30

Analysis: Turner-7

There is no reference to ceramics in the report on this mound (Willoughby and Hooton, 1922:77-78). The Peabody Museum catalogue, under numbers 30089-92, 30094, and with the specific provenience "lowest layer of ashes," does, however, list ceramics from this structure. Unfortunately, the plan and cross-section of the mound on page 78 of the published report, show no features that might correspond to such an ashbed. Furthermore, within the storage collection of the Museum, the box containing some of these sherds is labelled "Turner-11."

Scioto Series, McGraw Cord-marked—18
Body sherds, Grit: 17 (4- 7 mm; 5.0 mm)
Limestone: 1 (5 mm)

Scioto Series, McGraw Plain—14
Body sherds, Grit: 5 (4- 8 mm; 6.2 mm)
Limestone: 9 (3-14 mm; 5.5 mm)

Hopewellian Series, Chillicothe Rocker-stamped—5
A. Plain-rocked: 1 (Fig. 26, A)
Rim sherds, Grit: 1 (6 mm)
B. Plain long-rocked ("Pike"): 2
Body sherds, Grit: 2 (4.0 mm)
(zoned: 1)
D. Dentate-rocked: 2
Body sherds, Grit: 2 (4- 5 mm; 4.5 mm)
(zoned: 1)

Hopewellian Series, Untyped Zoned Incised—2
Body sherds, Grit: 1 (3 mm)
Limestone: 1 (5 mm)

Southeastern Series, Turner Check-stamped—1
Body sherds, Grit: 1 (5 mm)

Total 40 sherds

Comments

The same comments as those for Turner-1 apply to this mound as well. The distribution of the various ceramic series from Turner-7 is as follows:

	Percent	Sherds
Scioto Series:	80.00	32
Hopewellian Series:	17.50	7
Southeastern Series:	2.50	1

Within the Scioto Series (N = 32) the distribution of McGraw Cord-marked and McGraw Plain is as follows:

	Percent	Sherds
McGraw Cord-marked:	56.25	18
McGraw Plain:	43.75	14

The temper distribution for the total series is as follows:

	Percent	Sherds
Grit:	72.50	29
Limestone:	27.50	11

Analysis: Turner-9

The only reference to pottery in this mound is a brief comment in the site report to the effect that the "usual" flint chips and potsherds were scattered through the mound (Willoughby and Hooton, 1922:80). Data from the Peabody catalogue permit the identification of one sherd as coming from a "post hole under the mound" (No. 34508). The remaining material explicitly is assigned to the mound fill.

Unit-1: 34508

Hopewellian Series, Chillicothe Rocker-stamped—1
A. Plain-rocked: 1
Body sherds, Mixed: 1 (4 mm)

Unit-2: Mound Fill

Scioto Series, McGraw Cord-marked—25
Body sherds, Grit: 25 (3- 6 mm; 4.7 mm)

Scioto Series, McGraw Plain—5 (Fig. 26, B-C)
Body sherds, Grit: 3 (4- 8 mm; 6.3 mm)
Rim sherds, Grit: 1 (8 mm)
Limestone: 1 (3 mm)

Hopewellian Series, Chillicothe Rocker-stamped—5
A. Plain-rocked: 3
Body sherds, Limestone: 3 (4.0 mm)
C. Dentate long-rocked ("Pike"): 1 (Fig. 26, D, Pl. 42, *a*)
Rim sherds, Limestone: 1 (4 mm)
(zoned: 1)
D. Dentate-rocked: 1
Rim sherds, Limestone: 1 (4 mm)

Hopewellian Series, Chillicothe Brushed—1
Body sherds, Grit: 1 (4 mm)

Hopewellian Series, Indeterminate Residue—1
Body sherds, Grit: 1 (4 mm)
(zoned: 1)

PLATE 42

Turner-9. (*a* = unit-2) Chillicothe Rocker-stamped, dentate long-rocked.

PLATE 43

Turner Embankment. (*a*) Hopewell Rim; (*b*) Chillicothe Rocker-stamped, plain-rocked; (*c–d*) Miami Series, Untyped Punctate.

Southeastern Series, Turner Simple-stamped *A*—1
Body sherds, Limestone: 1 (4 mm)
(tetrapod: 1)

Southeastern Series, Turner Check-stamped—8
Body sherds, Limestone: 8 (4- 6 mm; 5.1 mm)

Miami Series, Untyped Embossed—1
Body sherds, Grit: 1 (4 mm)

Total 48 sherds

Comments

The same comments as those for Turner-1 apply to this mound as well. The distribution of the various ceramic series from Turner-9 is as follows:

	Percent	Sherds
Scioto Series:	62.50	30
Hopewellian Series:	16.66	8
Southeastern Series:	18.75	9
Miami Series:	2.08	1

Within the Scioto Series (N = 30) the distribution of McGraw Cord-marked and McGraw Plain is as follows:

	Percent	Sherds
McGraw Cord-marked:	83.33	25
McGraw Plain:	16.66	5

The temper distribution for the total series is as follows:

	Percent	Sherds
Grit:	66.66	32
Limestone:	31.25	15
Mixed:	2.08	1

Analysis: Turner-12

According to the published report on this structure (Willoughby and Hooton, 1922:80-85), the excavators "... failed to discover a single potsherd .... " from the entire mound. On the other hand, three sherds from this structure are listed in the Peabody Museum catalogue under number 30147; the provenience unit is given as "from refuse pile in center of mound."

Scioto Series; McGraw Cord-marked—2
Body sherds, Grit: 1 (4 mm)
Limestone: 1 (5 mm)

Scioto Series, McGraw Plain—1
Body sherds, Grit: 1 (--)

Total 3 sherds

Analysis: Turner site

The materials referred to under this heading were excavated not from the mounds, but from the cemetery within the great enclosure, and from the trenches cut into the earthwork embankments. The report of these excavations is contained in the Turner monograph by Willoughby and Hooton (1922:6-28).

A. Trenches in the Great Embankment

The great embankment is oval in shape, and encloses most of the mounds as well as the cemetery area. Four trenches in groups of two were cut through this structure. Trenches *A* and *B* (I and II in the Peabody catalogue) are in the southwestern section of the earthwork, just north of its junction with the graded way. Trenches *C* and *D* (III and IV in the Peabody catalogue) are at the northern extremity, northwest of the entrance to the structure.

References to pottery are scanty in the published report. For Trench *A*, which yielded several "altars," ash beds, post holes, a hearth, and several pits, it is merely noted that some of the pits produced potsherds (Willoughby and Hooton, 1922:8). For Trenches *B* and *C* no pottery is mentioned; for Trench *D* it is merely stated that among other things pottery was found (p. 13).

There is a distinct possibility that the trench numbering system in the catalogue does not follow the order of lettering in the published report. The reason for this is the reference in the catalogue under sherd numbers A-387 and A-390 indicating that the specimens were found in association with burials 2 and 3. The presumably equivalent Trench *A* of the published report did, however, yield no burials. On the other hand, burials did occur in Trenches *C* and *D*. It is therefore suggested that the trench numbers were reversed at the time of publication. Another disturbing aspect here, is that according to the published report, Trench *D* yielded pottery, whereas the ample collections in the Peabody Museum do not support these assertions; there are no sherds from Trench IV (*D*).

In view of this confusing situation it may be best to lump all the material from the embankment, regardless of individual trenches. In any case, stated associations in the catalogue are, for the most part, vague, being generally restricted to the trench number, and to such data as "from ash bed 1" or "from Section 13." In view of the general provenience of the finds here from a very homogeneous structure, one may perhaps assume general contemporaneity for all the materials buried within this rather low embankment.

Finally, in the pottery section of the Turner report, there are two brief references to ceramics from the embankment. First, on Plate 22, *c* a vessel of Brangenberg type is illustrated. Second, with reference to rocker-stamping it is stated that sherds thus decorated were found--*inter alia*—" . . . beneath the embankment of the great enclosure" (Willoughby and Hooton, 1922:92).

Scioto Series, McGraw Cord-marked—620 (Fig. 27, A-M, O)
Body sherds, Grit: 377 (3-12 mm; 5.5 mm)
Limestone: 212 (3-12 mm; 5.5 mm)
Rim sherds, Grit: 26 (4- 8 mm; 5.6 mm)
Limestone: 5 (5- 8 mm; 6.7 mm)

Scioto Series, McGraw Plain—259 (Fig. 28, A-Q)
Body sherds, Grit: 137 (4-12 mm; 6.5 mm)
Limestone: 83 (5-12 mm; 7.3 mm)
Rim sherds, Grit: 24 (4-12 mm; 7.8 mm)
Limestone: 15 (4-10 mm; 6.0 mm)

Hopewellian Series, Chillicothe Rocker-stamped—126
A. Plain-rocked: 35 (Pl. 43, *b*)
Body sherds, Grit: 18 (3- 5 mm; 4.1 mm)
Limestone: 17 (3- 5 mm; 4.0 mm)
(zoned: 5; lobed: 1)
B. Plain long-rocked ("Pike"): 28
Body sherds, Grit: 11 (4- 6 mm; 5.1 mm)
Limestone: 17 (4- 6 mm; 4.8 mm)
C. Dentate long-rocked ("Pike"): 20
Body sherds, Grit: 10 (3- 6 mm; 4.3 mm)
Limestone: 8 (4- 5 mm; 4.5 mm)
(zoned: 1)
Rim sherds, Limestone: 2 (4.0 mm)
D. Dentate-rocked: 43
Body sherds, Grit: 24 (4- 6 mm; 4.7 mm)
Limestone: 18 (3- 7 mm; 3.7 mm)
(zoned: 20; lobed: 7)
Rim sherds, Grit: 1 (6 mm)

Hopewellian Series, Chillicothe Brushed—1
Rim sherds, Limestone: 1 (6 mm)

Hopewellian Series, Chillicothe Incised—1 (Fig. 28, V)
Rim sherds, Limestone: 1 (6 mm)

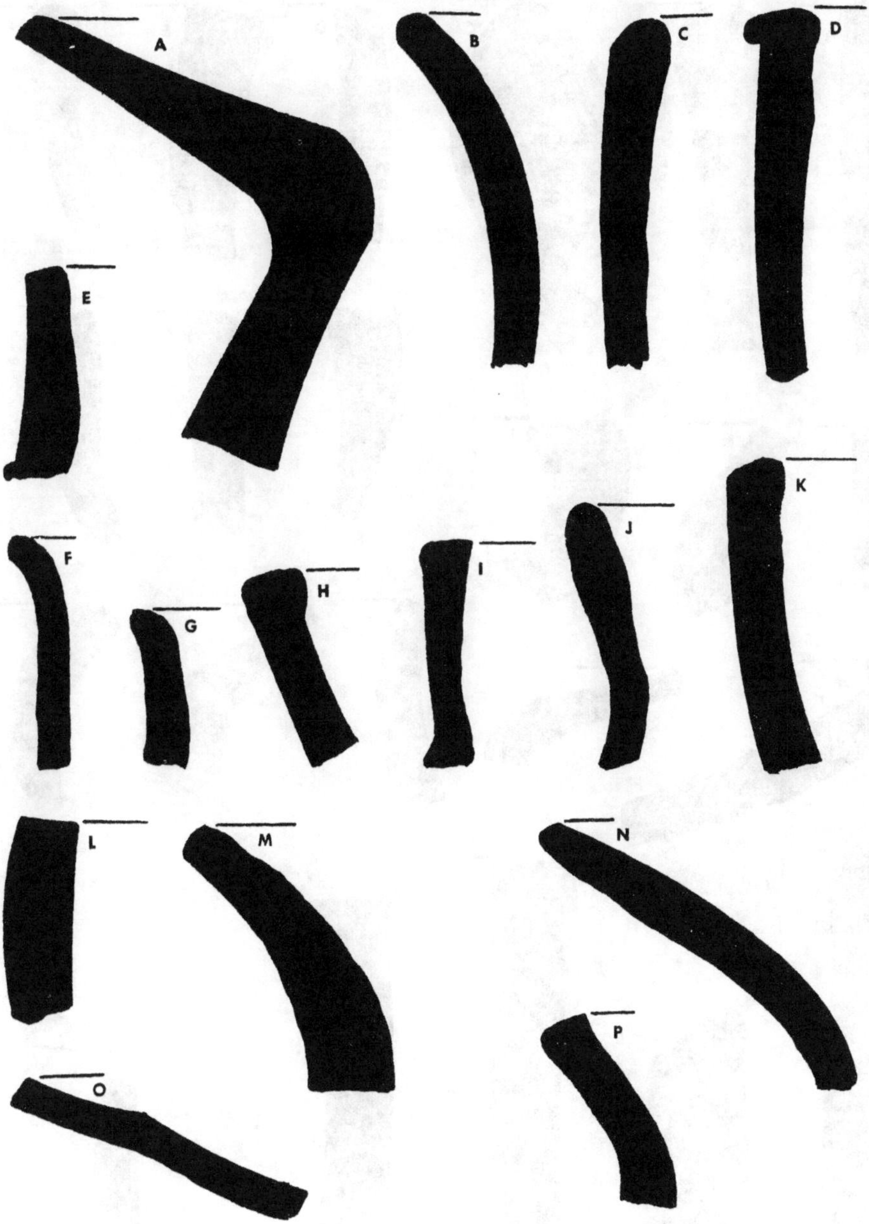

Fig. 27. Turner Embankment. (A-M,O) McGraw Cord-marked; (N, P) Turner Simple-stamped *B*.

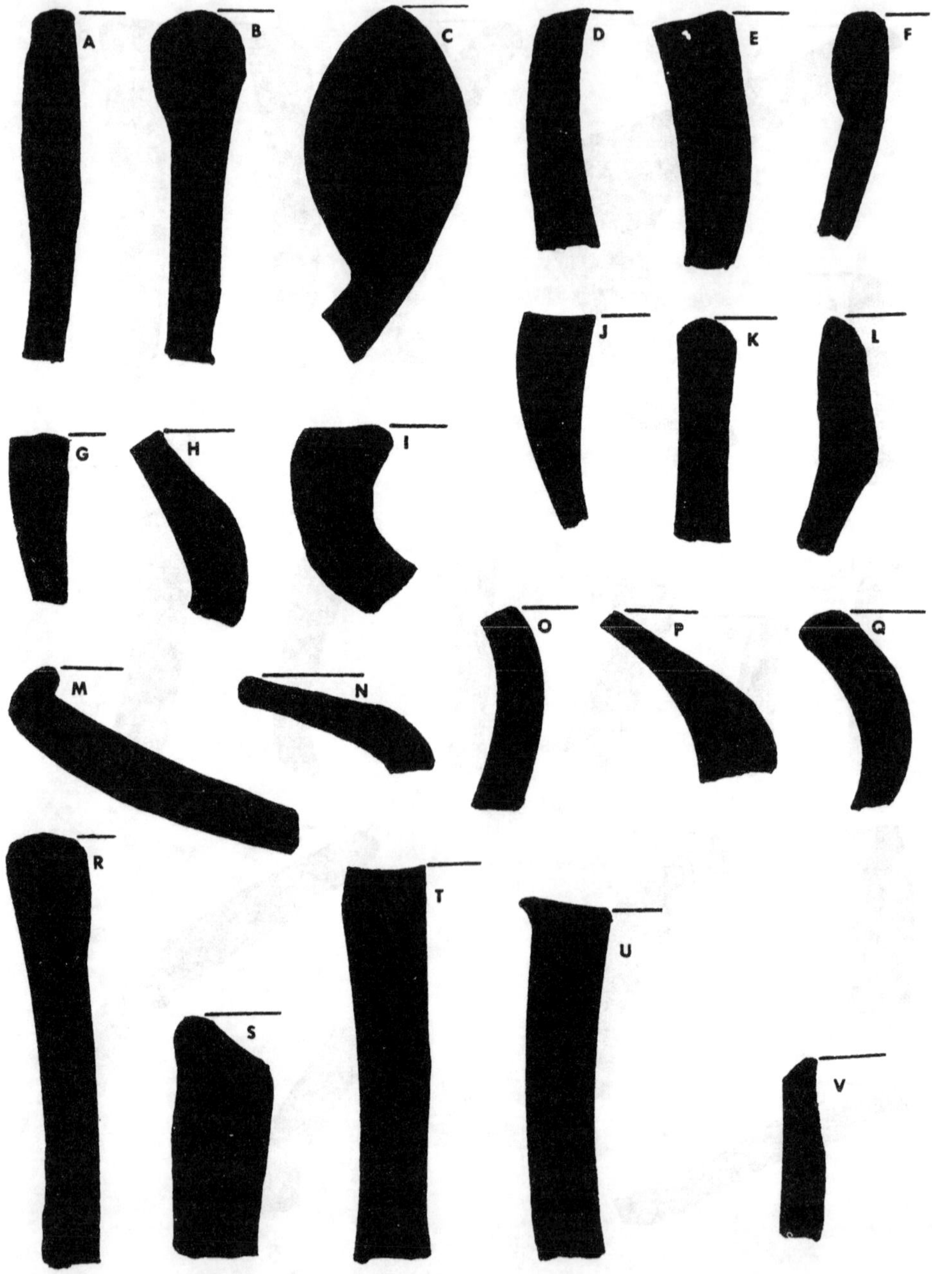

Fig. 28. Turner Embankment. (A–Q) McGraw Plain; (R–U) Miami Series, Punctate; (V) Chillicothe Incised.

Hopewellian Series, Brangenberg Plain—3
Rim sherds, Limestone: 3 (7-11 mm; 9.3 mm)

Hopewellian Series, Seip Plain—1
Body sherds, Limestone: 1 (4 mm)

Hopewellian Series, Untyped Zoned Incised—2
Body sherds, Grit: 2 (4- 7 mm; 5.5 mm)

Hopewellian Series, Hopewell Rims—22 (Pl. 43, *a*)
Grit: 11 (4- 6 mm; 5.2 mm)
Limestone: 11 (4- 6 mm; 5.4 mm)

Hopewellian Series, Indeterminate Residue—14
Body sherds, Grit: 11 (4- 6 mm; 5.1 mm)
Limestone: 3 (3- 5 mm; 4.0 mm)
(zoned: 10)

Southeastern Series, Turner Simple-stamped *A*—3
Body sherds, Grit: 2 (3.0 mm)
Limestone: 1 (9 mm)

Southeastern Series, Turner Simple-stamped *B*—15 (Fig. 27, N, P)
Body sherds, Sand: 13 (4- 7 mm; 4.8 mm)
Rim sherds, Sand: 2 (4- 6 mm; 5.0 mm)

Southeastern Series, Turner Check-stamped—13
Body sherds, Grit: 5 (4.0 mm)
Limestone: 8 (4- 6 mm; 4.8 mm)

Southeastern Series, Untyped Plain—18
Body sherds, Grit: 13 (--)
(tetrapods: 13)
Limestone: 3 (--)
(tetrapods: 3)
Sand: 1 (4 mm)
Rim sherds, Sand: 1 (5 mm)

Miami Series, Untyped Punctate—4 (Fig. 28, R-U; Pl. 43, *c–d*)
Rim sherds, Grit: 2 (9-12 mm; 10.5 mm)
Limestone: 2 (9.0 mm)

Unknown Series, Untyped Zoned Cord-marked—1
Body sherds, Grit: 1 (3 mm)

Total 1107 sherds

Comments

While all comments made under Turner-1 apply to this area as well, it must once more be stressed, how poor the fabrics, and how poorly executed the decorations are on the Hopewellian Series sherds. Here, as well as at all other Turner localities, the morphological breakdown of the usually so distinct vessel forms within the various ceramic series (excluding the Southeastern Series) is apparent. In the Hopewellian Series rim sherds, which on morphological grounds are Scioto, are quite common.

The distribution of the various ceramic series from the Turner Embankment is as follows:

	Percent	Sherds
Scioto Series:	79.40	879
Hopewellian Series:	15.36	170
Southeastern Series:	4.78	53
Miami Series:	.36	4
Other:	.09	1

Within the Scioto Series (N=879) the distribution of McGraw Cord-marked and McGraw Plain is as follows:

	Percent	Sherds
McGraw Cord-marked:	70.55	620
McGraw Plain:	29.46	259

The temper distribution for the total series is as follows:

	Percent	Sherds
Grit:	61.33	679
Limestone:	37.12	411
Sand:	1.53	17

B. *Cemetery within the Great Enclosure*

This is the area within the great enclosure which yielded a number of stone cist graves, as well as several pits, post holes, etc. In the published report this is discussed, burial by burial, and feature by feature (Willoughby and Hooton, 1922:14-28). The documentation for ceramics is relatively good. Combined with the Peabody catalogue numbers, a few sherds can be identified as to their original associations. The following are the published data of relevance.

Grave 24 yielded "Two flint knives and a few potsherds . . . " (Willoughby and Hooton, 1922:19). The Peabody Museum collection material from this single burial contains one sherd, numbered A-762. Grave 4-*a* " . . . contained the skeleton of a child . . . near the top of the skull was a fragmentary pottery vessel" (Willoughby and Hooton, 1922:22). This vessel was traced in the collection under catalogue numbers A-543 and A-544. The grave here is referred to as Grave 4. A nearly complete vessel was found in Grave 9-*b* which contained the skeleton of an adult male. "Three inches from the skull lay a pottery vessel . . . . Within it was a unio shell spoon. Against the pot rested a large busycon shell vessel, and against this was a sheet of mica" (Willoughby and Hooton, 1922:24). This burial yielded, in addition, a variety of other classic Hopewell artifacts. The catalogue number for this Hopewellian Series vessel of extremely high quality, is A-17. In the site report the finds from this burial are illustrated on Plate 7, *c*.

In addition, the site report refers twice to finds of sherds from what are presumed to be cache-pits (pp. 22-23). These references could not be coordinated with the documented material in the Peabody catalogue, beyond the notations for numbers A-823 and A-817, which indicate that these sherds were found in a pit "south of the barn" and in "pit 3—space between fence and Turner's road." The ceramics from these locations will, however, be dealt with separately here. The remainder of the pottery from this general area appears to have come from "general diggings," and, perhaps, from the surface.

Unit-1: A-762

Scioto Series, McGraw Plain—1 (Fig. 26, F)
Rim sherds, Grit: 1 (5 mm)

Unit-2: A-543-544

Southeastern Series, Untyped Plain—1
Vessel, Sand: 1 (5 mm)

Unit-3: A-17

Hopewellian Series, Chillicothe Rocker-stamped—1
A. Plain-rocked: 1 (Pl. 45, *b*)
Vessel, Limestone: 1 (body: 5 mm; rim: 5 mm)

Unit-4: A-823

Scioto Series, McGraw Cord-marked—2
Body sherds, Grit: 1 (7 mm)
Limestone: 1 (5 mm)

Unit-5: A-817

Scioto Series, McGraw Cord-marked—1
Body sherds, Mixed: 1 (5 mm)

PLATE 44

Turner Cemetery. All unit-6. (*a*) McGraw Cord-marked; (*b–c,e–f*) Chillicothe Rocker-stamped, plain long-rocked ("Pike"); (*d,g*) Turner Simple-stamped *B*. (Photograph by Peabody Museum, Harvard University.)

PLATE 45

Turner Cemetery. (*a* = unit-6) Southeastern Series, Untyped Complicated-stamped; (*b* = unit-3) Chillicothe Rocker-stamped, plain-rocked. (Photograph by Peabody Museum, Harvard University.)

Unit-6: General Diggings

Scioto Series, McGraw Cord-marked—18 (Fig. 26, E; Pl. 44, *a*)
Body sherds, Grit: 2 (5- 7 mm; 5.5 mm)
Limestone: 14 (4- 8 mm; 5.5 mm)
Rim sherds, Limestone: 2 (12.0 mm)

Scioto Series, McGraw Plain—13
Body sherds, Grit: 4 (5- 6 mm; 5.5 mm)
Limestone: 9 (3- 9 mm; 5.0 mm)

Hopewellian Series, Chillicothe Rocker-stamped—14
A. Body sherds, Grit: 6 (3- 5 mm; 3.6 mm)
Limestone: 4 (3- 5 mm; 4.2 mm)
Rim sherds, Clay: 1 (7 mm)
Grit: 2 (6.0 mm)
C. Dentate long-rocked ("Pike"): 1
Body sherds, Limestone: 1 (3 mm)

Hopewellian Series, Chillicothe Brushed—2
Body sherds, Limestone: 2 (4.0 mm)

Southeastern Series, Turner Simple-stamped *B*—2 (Pl. 44, *d, g*)
Body sherds, Sand: 2 (6.0 mm)

Southeastern Series, Turner Check-stamped—33
Body sherds, Grit: 32 (3- 7 mm; 4.7 mm)
Limestone: 1 (4 mm)

Southeastern Series, Untyped Plain—1 (Fig. 26, G)
Rim sherds, Sand: 1 (4 mm)

Southeastern Series, Untyped Cord-marked—2
Body sherds, Sand: 2 (5- 6 mm; 5.5 mm)

Southeastern Series, Untyped Complicated-stamped—1 (Pl. 45, *a*)
Body sherds, Grit: 1 (5 mm)

Southeastern Series, Untyped Check-stamped with stamped dot in check—1
Rim sherds, Grit: 1 (body: 6 mm; rim: 4 mm)

Unknown Series, Exterior and Interior Cord-marked—2
Body sherds, Grit: 2 (14.0 mm)

Unknown Series, Untyped Incised Grooved—1 (Fig. 26, I)
Rim sherds, Grit: 1 (4 mm)

Total 96 sherds

Comments

All previously made comments to the Turner material apply here as well. The single nearly-complete vessel from Unit-3 is rather unusual at Turner, since its quality is very high, almost approaching Seip standards. This vessel is cylindrical, and has a flat bottom; the zoning is angular. The curious sherd of the Southeastern Series here classed as Complicated-stamped is covered with large check-stamping; in each check-stamp is a stamped dot, which appears to have been part of the paddle stamp design. I know of nothing similar from any other Hopewellian site.

The distribution of the various ceramic series from the Turner Cemetery is as follows:

	Percent	Sherds
Scioto Series:	36.45	35
Hopewellian Series:	17.71	17
Southeastern Series:	42.71	41
Other:	3.12	3

Within the Scioto Series (N = 35) the distribution of McGraw Cord-marked and McGraw Plain is as follows:

	Percent	Sherds
McGraw Cord-marked:	62.85	22
McGraw Plain:	37.14	13

The temper distribution for the total series is as follows:

	Percent	Sherds
Grit:	55.21	53
Limestone:	36.45	35
Sand:	6.25	5
Clay:	1.04	1
Mixed:	1.04	1

APPENDIX

There should further be included in the Turner ceramic series a number of sherds which are either referred to in the published report but could not be traced in the collection, or which were not accessible to the investigator at the time of the Turner ceramic analysis.

In the published discussion of Turner-11 there is a reference to a burial near the left hip of which a broken vessel was found (Willoughby and Hooton, 1922:80). This vessel is illustrated on Plate 22, *d*. It might be described as follows:

Untyped, Embossed
Vessel, Rim sherds: 1

On Plate 22, *b* a fragmentary vessel from the Cemetery area is illustrated. This could not be traced in the collection:

Hopewellian Series, Chillicothe Rocker-stamped
A. Plain, long-rocked ("Pike"): 1
Rim sherds: 1 (quadrilobate)

On Plate 22, *g* a plain lobed bowl is illustrated. This was found in the central fireplace of Mound-1. It could not be traced in the collection:

Scioto Series, McGraw Plain
Vessel: 1 (multilobate)

Finally, two sherds should be mentioned which were seen but not examined nor traced as to provenience.

Southeastern Series, Untyped Complicated-stamped
Body sherd: 1

Southeastern Series, Tetrapod
Plain: 1

Not included in the count, because the material could neither be traced nor seen on any illustration in the published report is a reference to pottery from Turner-15 (Willoughby and Hooton, 1922:87).

The total number of sherds from the Turner site examined in this analysis is 3385. Griffin (1945:241) has stated that the sample he examined included 70 per cent grit tempered and 29 per cent limestone tempered ware. He also states that the sample included 67 per cent cord-marked and 21 per cent plain sherds. The series here analyzed, however, showed that 45 per cent of all sherds are grit tempered and 51 per cent limestone tempered; furthermore, 59 per cent of the sherds are cord-marked, and 20 per cent plain. These discrepancies have to remain unexplained. It may however be worth mentioning that Griffin did not examine the Turner material at the Peabody Museum, but that he had the collection shipped to Columbus, Ohio, where the study was carried out (Griffin, 1945:240). I have commented on this elsewhere as follows: "It is entirely possible that Griffin did not obtain the total sample from Turner, which is stored in the basement of the Museum, distributed in many storage trays containing all kinds of objects from the Turner Site. It would have had to depend upon the conscientiousness of the individual preparing the dispatch of the ceramic collection whether all the material extant was actually sent to Columbus. The total collection from the Turner site is so vast that easily some boxes of ceramics could have been overlooked at the time" (Prufer and McKenzie, 1965:33). This may explain the discrepant results of the two analyses.

RUSSELL BROWN MOUNDS

The Russell Brown mounds are located just outside of the Harness Earthworks in Ross County, Ohio. Properly speaking they should be considered part of the Harness site; several mounds, notably Harness-4 really form part of this series of structures. However, Frank Soday, who excavated four of the Brown mounds in 1961 christened them after the present owner of the farm on which they are located. Three of these mounds yielded ceramics, and will therefore be considered here. The mounds yielded, in addition to pottery, very rich classic Hopewell materials; these will be published in the general site report in the near future. Meanwhile, the ceramics will here be considered *in toto*, but without a detailed breakdown as to precise within-mound provenience units. These data will be contained in the site report. I am satisfied that these small mounds represent single units each of which were constructed at one time. The ceramics would appear to represent sherds deposited at the time of the mound construction. The Brown mounds are of particular interest, since they have produced a series of radiocarbon dates of considerable significance. These dates are presented in the final section of this study.

Analysis: Russell Brown-1

Scioto Series, McGraw Cord-marked—40
  Body sherds, Grit: 40 (3- 7 mm; 4.9 mm)

Scioto Series, McGraw Plain—37 (Fig. 29, A-E)
  Body sherds, Grit: 29 (4-10 mm; 4.9 mm)
  Rim sherds, Grit: 8 (5- 8 mm; 6.2 mm)

Hopewellian Series, Chillicothe Rocker-stamped—44
  A. Plain-Rocked: 22
    Body sherds, Grit: 22 (3- 5 mm; 4.1 mm)
      (zoned: 6)
  D. Dentate-rocked: 22
    Body sherds, Grit: 22 (2- 5 mm; 4.2 mm)
      (zoned: 9)

Hopewellian Series, Chillicothe Brushed—5
  Body sherds, Grit: 5 (4- 5 mm; 4.4 mm)
    (zoned: 1)

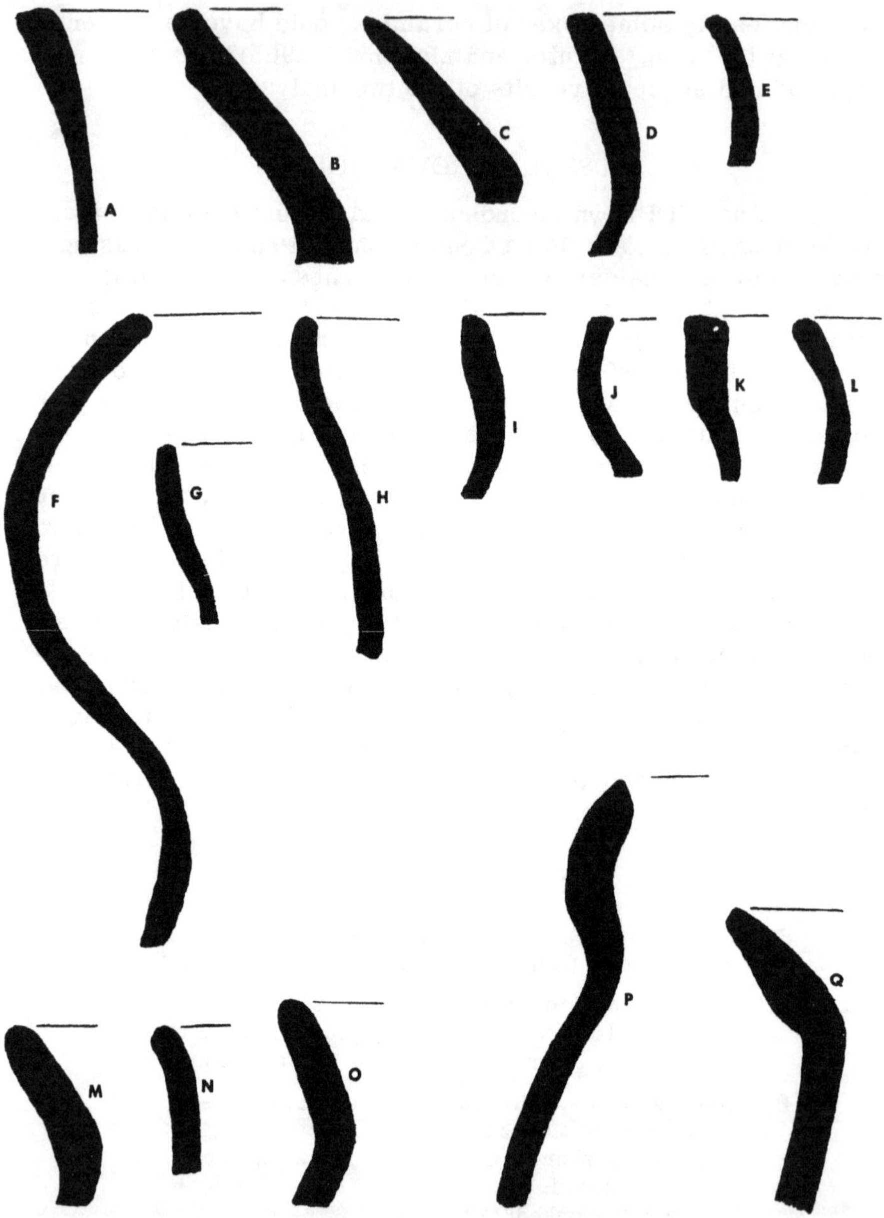

Fig. 29. Russell Brown-1. (A-E) McGraw Plain; (F) Bird Vessel; (G-K) Hopewell Rims; (L) Turner Simple-stamped *A*. Russell Brown-3. (M-O) McGraw Plain. Russell Brown-2. (P) Southeastern Series, Untyped Plain; (Q) Turner Simple-stamped *A*.

Hopewellian Series; Untyped Zoned Incised—26
Body sherds, Grit: 26 (4- 5 mm; 4.2 mm)

Hopewellian Series, Biglobular Bird vessels—2 (Fig. 29, F; Pl. 46, *a*)
Vessels, Grit: 2 (rims: 4.0 mm; bodies: 5.0 mm)

Hopewellian Series, Hopewell Rims—11 (Fig. 29, G-K)
Grit: 11 (3- 7 mm; 4.9 mm)

Hopewellian Series, Indeterminate Residue—13
Body sherds, Grit: 13 (3- 5 mm; 3.9 mm)
(zoned: 3)

Southeastern Series, Turner Simple-stamped *A*—36 (Fig. 29, L)
Body sherds, Grit: 34 (2- 5 mm; 3.1 mm)
Rim sherds, Grit: 2 (4.0 mm)

Southeastern Series, Untyped Cord-marked—1
Body sherds, Grit: 1 (5 mm)
(tetrapodal)

Southeastern Series, Turner Check-stamped—1
Body sherds, Grit: 1 (3 mm)

Southeastern Series, Untyped Plain—2
Body sherds, Grit: 2 (--)
(tetrapods: 2)

Uncertain Series, Indeterminate Residue—45
Body sherds, Grit: 45 (--)

Total 263 sherds

Comments

In the overall picture, three remarkable points should be stressed in this ceramic assemblage. First, and probably least important, is the great range of sherd color within and between the individual types. This ranges from black to buff; the Chillicothe Brushed sherds are all light grey. Second it should be stressed that this mound has yielded (in terms of reliable counts) the highest percentage of sherds of the Hopewellian Series, even after elimination of a number of sherds which proved to belong to the two reconstructable bird vessels. Finally, the two bird vessels are noteworthy. In all respects they are identical with the single specimen from the adjacent Harness-4 structure (see under Harness).

The Hopewellian Series material is, in every regard, of high quality. It compares very favorably with the material from Seip. The residual sherds are tiny, indeterminate fragments, probably belonging in the Scioto Series. The discrepancy between the

PLATE 46

Russell Brown-1. (*a*) Bird Vessel, zoned rocked dentate.

present sherd count and the brief statistic presented earlier (Prufer and McKenzie, 1965:31) is due to the following factors; As far as the Scioto Series is concerned a number of sherds could upon examination be fitted together and are now considered single sherds. Also some of the sherds listed as Scioto Series originally, are now classed under the heading Indeterminate Residue. The Hopewellian Series has substantially increased because additional materials have been submitted by the excavator since the original count was made. The same holds true for the Southeastern series.

The distribution of the various ceramic series from Russell Brown-1 is as follows:

	Percent	Sherds
Scioto Series:	29.27	77
Hopewellian Series:	38.40	101
Southeastern Series:	15.21	40
Other:	17.11	45

Within the Scioto Series (N = 77) the distribution of McGraw Cord-marked and McGraw Plain is as follows:

	Percent	Sherds
McGraw Cord-marked:	51.94	40
McGraw Plain:	48.05	37

All sherds are grit tempered, i.e. N = 100 per cent.

Analysis: Russell Brown-2

Scioto Series, McGraw Cord-marked—30
Body sherds, Grit: 30 (3- 7 mm; 5.0 mm)

Scioto Series, McGraw Plain—14
Body sherds, Grit: 14 (4-10 mm; 6.5 mm)

Hopewellian Series, Chillicothe Rocker-stamped—1
A. Plain-rocked: 1
Body sherds, Grit: 1 (6 mm)
(zoned: 1)

Hopewellian Series, Seip Plain—41
Body sherds, Grit: 41 (3- 5 mm; 4.0 mm)

Hopewellian Series, Hopewell Rims—1
Grit: 1 (5 mm)

Hopewellian Series, Indeterminate Residue—3
Body sherds, Grit: 2 (4- 5 mm; 4.5 mm)
Rim sherds, Grit: 1 (7 mm)

Southeastern Series, Turner Simple-stamped *A*—157 (Fig. 29, Q; Pl. 47)
Body sherds, Sandy grit: 153 (3- 7 mm; 5.0 mm)
Rim sherds, Sandy grit: 4 (6- 7 mm; 6.7 mm)

Southeastern Series, Untyped Plain—40 (Fig. 29, P)
Body sherds, Sand: 38 (4- 6 mm; 4.5 mm)
Rim sherds, Sand: 2 (8.0 mm)

Uncertain Series, Indeterminate Residue—77
Body sherds, Grit: 77 (--)

Total 364 sherds

Comments

The most outstanding aspect of the ceramics from Russell Brown-2 is the fact that the Southeastern Series is here represented by the highest percentage of the total ceramic assemblage ever encountered at an Ohio Hopewell site. A second feature of more than passing interest is that almost all sherds other than the straight sand tempered ones have a fair admixture of sand in their tempering material; this too is a unique characteristic of this site. The simple-stamped sherds here classed as Turner Simple-stamped *A* contain about 50 per cent sand. However, the nature of the stamping is sufficiently characteristic to qualify the material to be classed with Turner Simple-stamped *A*. The stamps are fairly wide, up to 3 mm for both ridges and depressions, and most of the sherds show some degree of smoothing. Most sherds, regardless of the series they belong to, but with the exception of Seip Plain, are crumbly and poorly fired. The Indeterminate Hopewell Rim cannot be identified beyond the presence of the punctates, as to the kind of decoration: the sherd is badly eroded. The residual sherds are tiny, unidentifiable fragments.

The distribution of the various ceramic series from Russell Brown-2 is as follows:

	Percent	Sherds
Scioto Series:	12.09	44
Hopewellian Series:	12.63	46
Southeastern Series:	54.12	197
Other:	21.15	77

Within the Scioto Series (N = 44) the distribution of McGraw Cord-marked and McGraw Plain is as follows:

	Percent	Sherds
McGraw Cord-marked:	68.18	30
McGraw Plain:	31.81	14

PLATE 47

a

Russell Brown-2. (*a*) Turner Simple-stamped-*A*.

The distribution of temper for the whole series is as follows:

	Percent	Sherds
Grit:	45.88	167
Sandy Grit:	43.13	157
Sand:	10.98	40

Analysis: Russell Brown-3

Scioto Series, McGraw Cord-marked—21
Body sherds, Grit: 21 (3- 7 mm; 5.0 mm)

Scioto Series, McGraw Plain—19 (Fig. 29, M-O)
Body sherds, Grit: 15 (3- 8 mm; 4.8 mm)
Rim sherds, Grit: 4 (5- 7 mm; 6.3 mm)

Hopewellian Series, Chillicothe Rocker-stamped—3
D. Dentate rocked: 3
Body sherds, Grit: 3 (4.0 mm)

Hopewellian Series, Indeterminate Residue—1
Body sherds, Grit: 1 (3 mm)

Southeastern Series, Turner Simple-stamped *A*—4
Body sherds, Grit: 4 (2- 4 mm; 3.0 mm)

Southeastern Series, Turner Simple-stamped *B*—3
Body sherds, Sand: 3 (4.0 mm)

Southeastern Series, Turner Check-stamped—2
Body sherds, Grit: 2 (2.0 mm)

Southeastern Series, Untyped Plain—2
Body sherds, Grit: 2 (--)
(tetrapods: 2)

Uncertain Series, Indeterminate Residue—7
Body sherds, Grit: 7 (--)

Total 62 sherds

Comments

In all respects the sherds listed for Russell Brown-3 conform to the type definitions. All the material is crumbly.

The distribution of the various ceramic series is as follows:

	Percent	Sherds
Scioto Series:	64.51	40
Hopewellian Series:	6.45	4
Southeastern Series:	17.74	11
Other:	11.29	7

Within the Scioto Series (N = 36) the distribution of McGraw Cord-marked and McGraw Plain is as follows:

	Percent	Sherds
McGraw Cord-marked:	47.22	21
McGraw Plain:	52.77	19

The temper distribution for the total series is as follows:

	Percent	Sherds
Grit:	95.16	59
Sand:	4.84	3

V

DISCUSSION

What conclusions can be drawn from the preceding detailed analysis of Ohio Hopewell pottery? Bearing in mind the limited reliability of the samples, any conclusions will, of necessity, have to be somewhat tentative. Still, in view of the fact that at least some of the collections are reasonably complete and adequately documented, the conclusions are, to my satisfaction, at least broadly acceptable. The ensuing discussion takes into account, (*a*) formal aspects of the ceramics, (*b*) relative chronology, and (*c*) absolute chronology. I have repeatedly dealt with the problem of Ohio Hopewell chronology (Prufer, 1963, 1964*a*, 1964*b*, 1965). The reader is referred to these publications for details regarding the chronological scheme arrived at in these studies, as well as for the rationale underlying division into Early, Middle, Late, and Latest Hopewell:

Latest Hopewell:	the hilltop enclosures.
Late Hopewell:	Turner, Marriott-1, McGraw, Brown's Bottom, Ginther, Newark, Marrietta.
Middle Hopewell:	Seip, Harness, Hopewell, Rockhold.
Early Hopewell:	Tremper, Mound City (at least certain mounds of this Group)

Other sites could not be reliably classified according to the criteria adopted. Others, again, such as the Brown Mounds, can only now be placed into the scheme, as a result of our recent analyses at Case Institute of Technology.

In the main, the present ceramic analysis confirms the above scheme in all essential points. At no time does it contradict the scheme, though in a number of instances it sheds no light on the problem either way. The following are the conclusions drawn from the evidence here analyzed:

1. Within the various ceramic series established, the material in the Scioto Series shows remarkable uniformity as far as morphology and dimensions are concerned. Based primarily upon the evidence from Tremper, and in a more limited way from Mound City, where provenience unit data are not adequate, McGraw Plain appears to be more common at early sites than at middle and late localities. Fort Hill may be an exception here, but on other grounds—the presence of Chillicothe Brushed sherds—this locality

ought to be very late in the sequence. Conceivably, the sample is inadequate; the plain sherds may merely represent one or two vessels the sherds of which were picked up in a few single locations. All indications point to the conclusion that sites which on other, non-ceramic grounds are late in the sequence, produced very large amounts of McGraw Cord-marked pottery and a few sherds of McGraw Plain; sites here would be McGraw, Turner, Marriott-1, Ginther, Ater, etc. The general tendency, from early to late, would appear to be reflected in decreasing quantities of McGraw Plain versus increasing amounts of McGraw Cord-marked. Certainly, it is true that Tremper, the earliest site by all available tests, produced almost exclusively McGraw Plain ceramics, while demonstrably late sites are dominated by McGraw Cord-marked.

While the quality of McGraw Cord-marked and McGraw Plain is, in the main, uniformly crumbly throughout, certain differences in this could occasionally be noted. Thus, at Turner, the poor quality of this material appears more in evidence than elsewhere, though here too variations were noted not only from mound to mound but also, for instance in the case of Turner-1, between provenience units within the same mound.

2. The Hopewellian Series proved to be the most sensitive ceramic series as far as change is concerned. In view of the previously established chronological framework, and in terms of extra-Ohio comparisons, these changes appear to have chronological significance. The earliest site, Tremper, produced no Hopewellian Series sherds whatever. At all other sites—even though in some cases the percentage distributions may be distorted because of the collecting and preservation habits of certain institutions in the past—Hopewellian ceramics constitute a distinct minority of the total ceramics. The unit of measurement for this statement is the individual mound or site, that is, not the specific within-mound provenience unit. Thus, at Rockhold-2 the Hopewellian Series constitutes 1.00 per cent of the total ceramic assemblage of 101 sherds. At the other end of the continuum, Seip-1, with a total of 428 sherds definitely assignable to that structure, had 40.18 per cent Hopewellian Series material; this, however, is an unreliable count because undoubtedly the bulk of the Scioto Series sherds as well as some other material listed under Seip-General came from Seip-1. The reliable maximum for the Hopewellian Series comes from Russell Brown-1, where the series is represented by 38.40 per cent. Generally speaking, the percentages of Hopewellian Series sherds cluster between 9 and 20 percent. The distribution does not seem to reflect a chronological tendency;

this is especially clear, because such late sites as Turner and McGraw, both of which are well documented, show a great discrepancy in this regard. At Turner, the major mounds and discrete areas (cemetery, embankment) show a range from 7.5 to 18.0 per cent for the Hopewellian Series, while at McGraw, this series participates only with 3.3 per cent in the total collection of 9,946 sherds.

The significant aspects of the Hopewellian Series through time are typological and qualitative. At early and middle sites of the Hopewellian Phase, the quality of the sherds is excellent. Fabrics are well-fired, and the decorations are carefully executed. At these sites too, vessel shapes with all their attributes, are quite distinct from those of other ceramic series, notably the Scioto Series. Seip, Mound City, Harness, and Hopewell can serve as examples for this situation. Here too, the typological range is more restricted. The Pike-related materials of the Chillicothe Rocker-stamped type are not in evidence. Similarly, Chillicothe Brushed and Chillicothe Incised are represented, if at all, only by a very few sherds.

At all late and latest sites, notably at McGraw, Turner, and Marriott-1, the fabrics of the Hopewellian Series sharply deteriorate. They are crumbly and poorly fired; in fact, they are virtually indistinguishable from those of the Scioto Series. Also, the morphological unity of the Hopewellian Series vessels now breaks down. Many vessels correspond in shape to vessels of the Scioto Series (Pl. 45,*b*). This is particularly apparent in the case of rim sherds; many of these are now flaring, bearing little or no resemblance to classic Hopewell Rims. Decorations also have deteriorated. They are carelessly applied, and often the dominant decorative element, rocker-stamping, is "wild" and overlapping. New types, and subtypes of the Chillicothe Rocker-stamped type, make their appearance. They have their parallels in Illinois Hopewell (Pike Rocker-stamped, Pike Scratched, and Baehr Brushed) where they are considered late within the local sequence. The general impression here is one of decline which elsewhere has been interpreted as evidence for pattern dissolution in Kroeber's sense of the word (Prufer and McKenzie, 1965).

In the Southeastern Series distribution no evidence could be found which might indicate chronological significance. At least Turner Simple-stamped *A* and *B* are present throughout the entire sequence. As a whole the series is invariably a minority component of the total ceramic assemblages, though occasionally a site with reliable sherd counts has produced more than 50 per cent of such material. The percentage range is from .44 per cent at

Marriott-1 to 54.12 per cent at Russell Brown-2. There is additional evidence that high percentages of Southeastern series sherds do at times appear; at the Turner Cemetery, 40.49 per cent of all ceramics (N = 95 sherds) belong here. At other Turner site components the range is from 2.50 to 18.75 per cent. By contrast, at the McGraw site, which ought to be about as old as Turner, the Southeastern Series is represented by only 1.00 per cent of the total ceramic assemblage. At Harness-4 and at the Edwin Harness Mound this series occurs in approximately equal proportions; the amounts run to 25.82 and 25.69 per cent respectively. No chronological trend can be isolated in the distribution of the Southeastern Series at Ohio sites.

The few sherds of the tentative Miami Series are almost exclusively restricted to the Turner site, where they were found in several of the component site units. In view of the fact that these sherds closely resemble the Illinoian Weaver ceramics, this concentration would seem to be further proof of the lateness of Turner within the Ohio Hopewellian Phase.

3. The distribution of tempering materials does not seem, with one exception, to have any particular significance. The exception is sand temper, which is invariably associated with sherds which in every identifiable case belong in the Southeastern Series. The bulk of the sherds from all sites are either grit or limestone tempered. On the whole, grit is predominant, though occasionally, such as at Turner, Tremper, and Mound City this is reversed. At Marriott-1 limestone is common. In fact, at certain Turner localities grit predominates, though in the over-all picture limestone is dominant. No chronological trend can be isolated for temper distribution.

4. Much has been written about the possible time range of the various mounds within a given mound group. Wherever the ceramic data proved to be adequate, no great temporal range for any given mound group seems to be indicated, with the possible exception of Harness, where radiocarbon dates for the Russell Brown Mounds associated with the site indicate a considerable time span. Here, however, the ceramics are too scanty to permit verification. Certainly, the presence of identical biglobular vessels at Harness-4 and Russell Brown-1 would seem to indicate that these two structures are very close in time.

At such sites as Turner and Seip the most remarkable evidence for possible temporal closeness of the various component mounds is indicated by the fundamental ceramic unity. At Turner especially—to which should be added the associated Marriott-1 mound—the ceramics from all units show the same qualitative and typological attributes which I have interpreted as being indicative of a general decline. This is the more interesting, since the provenience data for this material are unusually good. In a more limited sense this also applies to Seip, where the basic data are somewhat less excellent. Still, here too it is perfectly clear that the high quality of the ceramic material of the Hopewellian Series was characteristic of both mounds, and of the various units within Seip-1. At both sites, this seems to be indicative of a relatively short-lived period during which these ceremonial centers were operational.

At present, that is, without the evidence from the recently excavated Mound City locations, it would seem to me that the time span of this center may be somewhat longer than that of the two sites just discussed. I am reasonably certain that the mound excavated by Squier and Davis, which yielded the famed cache of "killed" platform pipes, must be nearly contemporaneous with Tremper which yielded a similar cache of almost identical attributes. On the other hand, a recent radiocarbon date for one of the structures excavated in 1963 has yielded a value of A.D. 178 ± 53 (OWU-51). This certainly would indicate a later phase of the site's occupation than that for the mound which yielded the pipe cache.

All that remains to be discussed is the absolute chronology of some of the sites dealt with in this report. Only one of the localities for which dates are available did not yield pottery; this is the West Mound in Ross County, Ohio. On the basis of the scanty data available, this structure would fall into the middle period of the Hopewellian Phase. The dates for the Hopewell-25 structure are somewhat problematical. Certainly, the 335 B.C. date should be eliminated since it is based on a composite shell sample scooped up from various areas on the floor of the mound. The other two dates may also be suspect, however; they are rather early Chicago dates and may not reflect true values. On purely artifactual grounds I would place this mound into Middle Hopewell, that is *circa* 100 to 150 years later than the youngest radiocarbon date. However, the rather large plus/minus values here, do in fact permit such a later attribution anyway. The following list of dates is self-explanatory. When viewed in the light of the preceding discussion of ceramics, it will be seen that the ceramic evidence to a large extent supports the independently established dates.

Site	Sample	Material	Date
Hopewell-25	C-137	shell	335 B.C. ± 210
Hopewell-25	C-139	bark	94 B.C. ± 250
Hopewell-25	C-136	charcoal	1 B.C. ± 200
Tremper	UCLA -290	charcoal	100 B.C. ± 100
Seip-1	UCLA -292	charcoal	55 A.D. ± 100
Mound City-10 . . .	OWU - 51	charcoal	178 A.D. ± 53
West	M-650	charcoal	60 A.D. ± 200
West	M-928	charcoal	120 A.D. ± 200
Russell Brown-1 . .	UCLA -244-A	charcoal	200 A.D. ± 80
Russell Brown-1 . .	UCLA -244-B	charcoal	140 B.C. ± 70
Russell Brown-2 . .	UCLA -245	charcoal	90 A.D. ± 90
Russell Brown-3 . .	UCLA -246-A	charcoal	615 A.D. ± 70
Russell Brown-3 . .	UCLA -246-B	charcoal	590 A.D. ± 70
Russell Brown-3 . .	UCLA -246-C	charcoal	430 A.D. ± 90
McGraw.	OWU - 61	charcoal	481 A.D. ± 65
McGraw.	OWU - 62	charcoal	435 A.D. ± 166
McGraw.	UCLA -679-A	charcoal	140 A.D. ± 80
McGraw.	UCLA -679-B	charcoal	190 A.D. ± 80
McGraw.	UCLA -679-C	charcoal	440 A.D. ± 80
McGraw.	UCLA -685	bone	230 B.C. ± 80
McGraw.	UCLA -688	charcoal	280 A.D. ± 80

The dates for Russell Brown-2 and 3 are the revised dates and not the faulty ones published by Fergusson and Libby (1963). On the basis of the evidence I believe that 140 B.C. (Sample-UCLA-244-B) for Russell Brown-1 is too old, and should therefore be disregarded; the A.D. 200 (Sample UCLA-244-A) date is more in line with the excavated remains. The McGraw dates have been discussec at length elsewhere (Prufer, 1965:102-4). Only UCLA-685 requires brief comment; this date is obviously unacceptable. It was run on a bone sample as an experiment in the development of a new method of dating bone and shell from their organic components (Berger, Horney, and Libby, 1964).

REFERENCES

Atwater, C.
1820 Description of the Antiquities Discovered in the State of Ohio and Other Western States. American Antiquarian Society, Archaeologia American, Transactions and Collections, 1:105-267. Worcester, Mass.

Baby, R. S., and J. A. Brown
1964 Re-Examination of the Mound City Group. Paper presented at the 29th Annual Meeting of the Society for American Archaeology, Chapel Hill, North Carolina.

Berger, R., A. G. Horney, and W. F. Libby
1964 Radiocarbon Dating of Bone and Shell from their Organic Components. Science, 144(3621):999-1001.

Blank, J. E.
1965 The Brown's Bottom Site, Ross County, Ohio. Ohio Archaeologist, 15(1):16-21.

Fergusson, G. J., and W. F. Libby
1963 UCLA Radiocarbon Dates II. Radiocarbon, 5:1-22. New Haven.

Greenman, E. F.
1930 Department of Archaeology. Ohio State Museum, Museum Echoes, 3(5):5.

Griffin, J. B.
1945 The Ceramic Affiliations of the Ohio Valley Adena Culture. *In:* Webb, W. S. and C. E. Snow, The Adena People. University of Kentucky, Reports in Anthropology and Archaeology, 6:220-46.

1952 Some Early and Middle Woodland Pottery Types in Illinois. *In:* Deuel, T., Hopewellian Communities in Illinois. Illinois State Museum, Scientific Papers, 5(3):93-129.

1958 The Chronological Position of the Hopewellian Culture in the Eastern United States. Anthropological Papers, Museum of Anthropology, University of Michigan, No. 12. Ann Arbor.

Griffin, J. B., and W. H. Sears
1950 Certain Sand-tempered Pottery Types of the Southeast. Prehistoric Pottery of the Eastern United States. Museum of Anthropology, University of Michigan, Ann Arbor.

Haag, W. G.
1942*a* The Pottery from the C and O Mounds at Paintsville. *In:* Webb, W. S., The C and O Mounds at Paintsville, Sites Jo 2 and Jo 9, Johnson County, Kentucky. University of Kentucky, Reports in Anthropology and Archaeology, 5(4):341-49.

1942*b* A Description and Analysis of the Pickwick Pottery. *In:* Webb, W. S., and D. L. DeJarnette, An Archeological Survey of Pickwick Basin in the Adjacent Portions of the States of Alabama, Mississippi and Tennessee. Bureau of American Ethnology, Bulletin 129:509-26.

Johnson, Elden
1962 The Prehistory of the Red River Valley. Minnesota History, V. 38:146-55.

Mills, W. C.
1907 The Exploration of the Edwin Harness Mound. Ohio State Archaeological and Historical Quarterly, No. 16:113-93.

1909 Exploration of the Seip Mound. *Ibid.* No. 18:269-321.

1912 Archaeological Remains of Jackson County. *Ibid.* No. 21:175-214.

1916 Exploration of the Tremper Mound. *Ibid.* No. 25:262-398.

1922 Exploration of the Mound City Group. *Ibid.* No. 31:423-584.

Moorehead, W. K.
1890 Fort Ancient, the Great Prehistoric Earthwork of Warren County, Ohio, Compiled from a Careful Survey, With an Account of its Mounds and Graves. Cincinnati: R. Clarge & Co.

1897 Report of Fieldwork, Carried out in the Muskingum, Scioto, and Ohio Valley during the Season of 1896. Ohio State Archaeological and Historical Quarterly, 5:165-274.

1908 Fort Ancient, the Great Prehistoric Earthwork of Warren County, Ohio. Phillips Academy, Department of Archaeology, Bulletin 4:27-166. Andover, Mass.

1922 The Hopewell Mound Group of Ohio. Field Museum of National History, Publication 211 (Anthropological Series, 4(5):73-181). Chicago.

Morgan, R. G.
1960 Fort Ancient. Ohio State Archaeological and Historical Society. Columbus.

Morgan, R. G., and E. S. Thomas
1948 Fort Hill. *Ibid.*

Phillips. P., J. A. Ford, and J. B. Griffin
1951 Archaeological Survey in the Lower Mississippi Valley, 1940-1947. Harvard University, Peabody Museum of American Archaeology and Ethnology, Papers, 25.

Prufer, O. H.
1963 Der Hopewell-Komplex der Östlichen Vereinigten Staaten. Paideuma, 9(2): 122-47. Frankfurt.

1964*a* The Hopewell Complex of Ohio. Illinois State Museum, Scientific Papers, 12(2):35-83.

1964*b* The Hopewell Cult. Scientific American, 211(6):90-102.

1965 The McGraw Site: A Study in Hopewellian Dynamics. Cleveland Museum of Natural History, Scientific Publications, 4(1):1-142.

Prufer, O. H., and D. H. McKenzie

1965 Ceramics. *In*: Prufer, O. H., The McGraw Site: A Study in Hopewellian Dynamics. Cleveland Museum of Natural History, Scientific Publications, 4(1):16-57.

Putnam, F. W.

1886*a* Report of the Curator. Harvard University, Peabody Museum of American Archaeology and Ethnology, 18th Annual Report, *In:* Reports of the Peabody Museum, (1887), 3(5):401-18.

1886*b* The Marriott Mound No. 1, and its Contents. Harvard University, Peabody Museum of American Archaeology and Ethnology, 18th Annual Report. *In:* Reports of the Peabody Museum, (1887), 3(5):449-66.

Shetrone, H. C.

1925 Exploration of the Ginther Mound; the Miesse Mound. Ohio State Archaeological and Historical Quarterly, No. 34:154-68.

1926 Exploration of the Hopewell Group of Prehistoric Earthworks. *Ibid.* No. 35:1-227.

Shetrone, H. C., and E. F. Greenman

1931 Explorations of the Seip Group of Prehistoric Earthworks. *Ibid.* 40:343-509.

Squier, E. G., and E. H. Davis

1848 Ancient Monuments of the Mississippi Valley. Smithsonian Institution, Contributions to Knowledge, 1. Washington.

Starr, S. F.

1960 Archaeology of Hamilton County, Ohio. Cincinnati Museum of Natural History Journal, 23(1):1-130.

Willoughby, C. C., and E. A. Hooton

1922 The Turner Group of Earthworks, Hamilton County, Ohio. Harvard University, Peabody Museum of American Archaeology and Ethnology, Papers, 8(3).

www.ingramcontent.com/pod-product-compliance
Lightning Source LLC
LaVergne TN
LVHW050022250826
846302LV00008B/55